C-2420

ISBN 0-8373-2420-3

THE PASSBOOK® SERIES

PASSBOOKS®

FOR

CAREER OPPORTUNITIES

CHIEF EXCISE TAX INVESTIGATOR

National Learning Corporation

212 Michael Drive, Syosset, New York 11791

(516) 921-8888

National Learning Corporation

212 Michael Drive, Syosset, New York 11791
(516) 921-8888

PRINTED IN THE UNITED STATES OF AMERICA

PASSBOOK®

NOTICE

This book is *SOLELY* intended for, is sold *ONLY* to, and its use is *RESTRICTED* to *individual*, bona fide applicants or candidates who qualify by virtue of having seriously filed applications for appropriate license, certificate, professional and/or promotional advancement, higher school matriculation, scholarship, or other legitimate requirements of educational and/or governmental authorities.

This book is *NOT* intended for use, class instruction, tutoring, training, duplication, copying, reprinting, excerption, or adaptation, etc., by:

(1) Other Publishers
(2) Proprietors and/or Instructors of "Coaching" and/or Preparatory Courses
(3) Personnel and/or Training Divisions of commercial, industrial, and governmental organizations
(4) Schools, colleges, or universities and/or their departments and staffs, including teachers and other personnel
(5) Testing Agencies or Bureaus
(6) Study groups which seek by the purchase of a single volume to copy and/or duplicate and/or adapt this material for use by the group as a whole without having purchased individual volumes for each of the members of the group
(7) Et al.

Such persons would be in violation of appropriate Federal and State statutes.

PROVISION OF LICENSING AGREEMENTS. — Recognized educational commercial, industrial, and governmental institutions and organizations, and others legitimately engaged in educational pursuits, including training, testing, and measurement activities, may address a request for a licensing agreement to the copyright owners, who will determine whether, and under what conditions, including fees and charges, the materials in this book may be used by them. In other words, a licensing facility *exists* for the legitimate use of the material in this book on other than an individual basis. However, it is asseverated and affirmed here that the materials in this book *CANNOT* be used without the receipt of the express permission of such a licensing agreement from the Publishers.

NATIONAL LEARNING CORPORATION
212 Michael Drive
Syosset, New York 11791

Inquiries re licensing agreements should be addressed to:
The President
National Learning Corporation
212 Michael Drive
Syosset, New York 11791

PASSBOOK SERIES®

THE *PASSBOOK SERIES®* has been created to prepare applicants and candidates for the ultimate academic battlefield—the examination room.

At some time in our lives, each and every one of us may be required to take an examination—for validation, matriculation, admission, qualification, registration, certification, or licensure.

Based on the assumption that every applicant or candidate has met the basic formal educational standards, has taken the required number of courses, and read the necessary texts, the *PASSBOOK SERIES®* furnishes the one special preparation which may assure passing with confidence, instead of failing with insecurity. Examination questions—together with answers—are furnished as the basic vehicle for study so that the mysteries of the examination and its compounding difficulties may be eliminated or diminished by a sure method.

This book is meant to help you pass your examination provided that you qualify and are serious in your objective.

The entire field is reviewed through the huge store of content information which is succinctly presented through a provocative and challenging approach—the question-and-answer method.

A climate of success is established by furnishing the correct answers at the end of each test.

You soon learn to recognize types of questions, forms of questions, and patterns of questioning. You may even begin to anticipate expected outcomes.

You perceive that many questions are repeated or adapted so that you gain acute insights, which may enable you to score many sure points.

You learn how to confront new questions, or types of questions, and to attack them confidently and work out the correct answers.

You note objectives and emphases, and recognize pitfalls and dangers, so that you may make positive educational adjustments.

Moreover, you are kept fully informed in relation to new concepts, methods, practices, and directions in the field.

You discover that you are actually taking the examination all the time: you are preparing for the examination by "taking" an examination, not by reading extraneous and/or supererogatory textbooks.

In short, this PASSBOOK®, used directedly, should be an important factor in helping you to pass your test.

CHIEF EXCISE TAX INVESTIGATOR

DUTIES

As a Chief Excise Tax Investigator, you would direct and supervise a unit of subordinate investigators engaged in enforcing the Petroleum, Alcohol and Tobacco Tax Laws. You would be in charge of assigning and coordinating field investigations, surveillances, seizures and arrests made by excise tax investigators. You would either supervise subordinate excise tax investigators, or independently conduct the more complex investigations. Perform related duties.

SUBJECT OF EXAMINATION

The written test will be designed to test for knowledge, skills, and/or abilities in such areas as:

1. Advanced investigative techniques;
2. Court-related investigative techniques;
3. Evaluating information and evidence;
4. Preparing written material;
5. Understanding and interpreting written material;
6. Administrative supervision; and
7. Administration.

HOW TO TAKE A TEST

I. YOU MUST PASS AN EXAMINATION

A. WHAT EVERY CANDIDATE SHOULD KNOW

Examination applicants often ask us for help in preparing for the written test. What can I study in advance? What kinds of questions will be asked? How will the test be given? How will the papers be graded?

As an applicant for a civil service examination, you may be wondering about some of these things. Our purpose here is to suggest effective methods of advance study and to describe civil service examinations.

Your chances for success on this examination can be increased if you know how to prepare. Those "pre-examination jitters" can be reduced if you know what to expect. You can even experience an adventure in good citizenship if you know why civil service examinations are given.

B. WHY ARE CIVIL SERVICE EXAMINATIONS GIVEN?

Civil service examinations are important to you in two ways. As a citizen, you want public jobs filled by employees who know how to do their work. As a job-seeker, you want a fair chance to compete for that job on an equal footing with other candidates. The best known means of accomplishing this two-fold goal is the competitive examination.

Examinations are widely publicized throughout the nation. They may be administered for jobs in federal, state, city, municipal, town, or village governments or agencies.

Any citizen may apply, with some limitations, such as the age or residence of applicants. Your experience and education may be reviewed to see whether you meet the requirements for the particular examination. When these requirements exist, they are reasonable and are applied consistently to all applicants. Thus, a competitive examination may cause you some uneasiness now, but it is your privilege and safeguard.

C. HOW ARE CIVIL SERVICE EXAMINATIONS DEVELOPED?

Examinations are carefully written by trained technicians who are specialists in the field known as "psychological measurement," in consultation with recognized authorities in the field of work that the test will cover. These experts recommend the subject matter areas or skills to be tested; only those knowledges or skills important to your success on the job are included. The most reliable books and source materials available are used as references. Together, the experts and technicians judge the difficulty level of the questions.

Test technicians know how to phrase questions so that the problem is clearly stated. Their ethics do not permit "trick" or "catch" questions. Questions may have been tried out on sample groups, or subjected to statistical analysis, to determine their usefulness.

Written tests are often used in combination with performance tests, ratings of training and experience, and oral interviews. All of these measures combine to form the best known means of finding the right man for the right job.

II. HOW TO PASS THE WRITTEN TEST

A. *NATURE OF THE EXAMINATION*

To prepare intelligently for civil service examinations, you should know how they differ from school examinations you have taken. In school you were assigned certain definite pages to read or subjects to cover. The examination questions were quite detailed and usually emphasized memory. Civil service examinations, on the other hand, try to discover your present ability to perform the duties of a position, plus your potentiality to learn these duties. In other words, a civil service examination attempts to predict how successful you will be. Questions cover such a broad area that they cannot be as minute and detailed as school examination questions.

In the public service similar kinds of work, or positions, are grouped together in one "class." This process is known as "position-classification." All the positions in a class are paid according to the salary range for that class. One class title covers all these positions, and they are all tested by the same examination.

B. *FOUR BASIC STEPS*

1. Study the Announcement.--How, then, can you know what subjects to study? Our best answer is: "Learn as much as possible about the class of positions for which you have applied." The examination will test the knowledge, skills, and abilities needed to do the work.

Your most valuable source of information about the position you want is the official announcement of the examination. This announcement lists the training and experience qualifications. Check these standards and apply only if you come reasonably close to meeting them.

The brief description of the position in the examination announcement offers some clues to the subjects which will be tested. Think about the job itself. Review the duties in your mind. Can you perform them, or are there some in which you are rusty? Fill in the blank spots in your preparation.

Many jurisdictions preview the written test in the examination announcement by including a section called "Knowledge and Abilities Required," "Scope of Examination," or some similar heading. Here you will find out specifically what fields will be tested.

2. Review Your Own Background.-- Once you learn in general what the position is all about, and what you need to know to do the work, ask yourself which subjects you already know fairly well and which need improvement. You may wonder whether to concentrate on improving your strong areas or on building some background in your fields of weakness. When the announcement has specified "some knowledge" or "considerable knowledge," or has used adjectives such as "beginning principles of ...." or "advanced .....methods," you can get a clue as to the number and difficulty of questions to be asked in any given field. More questions, and hence broader coverage, would be included for those subjects which are more important in the work. Now weigh your strengths and weaknesses against the job requirements and prepare accordingly.

3. Determine the Level of the Position.-- Another way to tell how intensively you should prepare is to understand the level of the job for which you are applying. Is it the entering level? In other words, is this the position in which beginners in a field of work are hired? Or is it an intermediate or advanced level? Sometimes this is indicated by such words as "Junior" or "Senior" in the class title.Other jurisdictions use Roman numerals to designate the level: Clerk I,

Clerk II, for example. The word "Supervisor" sometimes appears in the title. If the level is not indicated by the title, check the description of duties. Will you be working under very close supervision, or will you have responsibility for independent decisions in this work?

4. Choose Appropriate Study Materials.-- Now that you know the subjects to be examined and the relative amount of each subject to be covered, you can choose suitable study materials. For beginning level jobs, or even advanced ones, if you have a pronounced weakness in some aspect of your training, read a modern, standard textbook in that field. Be sure it is up-to-date and has general coverage. Such books are normally available at your library, and the librarian will be glad to help you locate one. For entry level positions, questions of appropriate difficulty are chosen -- neither highly advanced questions, nor those too simple. Such questions require careful thought but not advanced training.

If the position for which you are applying is technical or advanced, you will read more advanced, specialized material. If you are already familiar with the basic principles of your field, elementary textbooks would waste your time. Concentrate on advanced textbooks and technical periodicals. Think through the concepts and review difficult problems in your field.

These are all general sources. You can get more ideas on your own initiative, following these leads. For example, training manuals and publications of the government agency which employs workers in your field can be useful, particularly for technical and professional positions. A letter or visit to the government department involved may result in more specific study suggestions, and certainly will provide you with a more definite idea of the exact nature of the position you are seeking.

III. KINDS OF TESTS

Tests are used for purposes other than measuring knowledge and ability to perform specified duties. For some positions, it is equally important to test ability to make adjustments to new situations or to profit from training. In others, basic mental abilities not dependent upon information are essential. Questions which test these things may not appear as pertinent to the duties of the position as those which test for knowledge and information. Yet they are often highly important parts of a fair examination. For very general questions, it is almost impossible to help you direct your study efforts. What we can do is to point out some of the more common of these general abilities needed in public service positions and describe some typical questions.

1. General Information

Broad, general information has been found useful for predicting job success in some kinds of work. This is tested in a variety of ways, from vocabulary lists to questions about current events. Basic background in some field of work, such as sociology or economics, may be sampled in a group of questions. Often these are principles which have become familiar to most persons through "exposure" rather than through formal training. It is difficult to advise you how to study for these questions; being alert to the world around you is our best suggestion.

2. Verbal Ability

An example of an ability needed in many positions is verbal or language ability. Verbal ability is, in brief, the ability to use and understand words. Vocabulary and grammar tests are typical measures of this ability. "Reading comprehension" or "paragraph interpretation" questions are common in many kinds of civil service tests. You are given a paragraph of written material and asked to find its central meaning.

3. Numerical Ability

Number skills can be tested by the familiar arithmetic problem, by checking paired lists of numbers to see which are alike and which are different, or by interpreting charts and graphs. In the latter test, a graph may be printed in the test booklet which you are asked to use as the basis for answering questions.

4. Observation

A popular test for law-enforcement positions is the observation test. A picture is shown to you for several minutes, then taken away. Questions about the picture test your ability to observe both details and larger elements.

5. Following Directions

In many positions in the public service, the employee must be able to carry out written instructions dependably and accurately. You may be given a chart with several columns, each column listing a variety of information. The questions require you to carry out directions involving the information given in the chart.

6. Skills and Aptitudes

Performance tests effectively measure some manual skills and aptitudes. When the skill is one in which you are trained, such as typing or shorthand, you can practice. These tests are often very much like those given in business school or high school courses. For many of the other skills and aptitudes, however, no short-time preparation can be made. Skills and abilities natural to you or that you have developed throughout your lifetime are being tested.

Many of the general questions just described provide all the data needed to answer the questions and ask you to use your reasoning ability to find the answers. Your best preparation for these tests, as well as for tests of facts and ideas, is to be at your physical and mental best. You, no doubt, have your own methods of getting into an exam-taking mood and keeping "in shape." The next section lists some ideas on this subject.

IV. KINDS OF QUESTIONS

Only rarely is the "essay" question, which you answer in narrative form, used in civil service tests. Civil service tests are usually of the short-answer type. Full instructions for answering these questions will be given to you at the examination. But in case this is your first experience with short-answer questions and separate answer sheets, here is what you need to know.

1. Multiple-Choice Questions

Most popular of the short-answer questions is the "multiple-choice" or "best-answer" question. It can be used, for example, to test for factual knowledge, ability to solve problems, or judgment in meeting situations found at work.

A multiple-choice question is normally one of three types:

(1) It can begin with an incomplete statement followed by several possible endings. You are to find the one ending which *best* completes the statement, although some of the others may not be entirely wrong.

(2) It can also be a complete statement in the form of a question which is answered by choosing one of the statements listed.

(3) It can be in the form of a problem -- again you select the best answer.

Here is an example of a multiple-choice question with a discussion which should give you some clues as to the method for choosing the right answer.

SAMPLE QUESTION:

When an employee has a complaint about his assignment, the action which will *best* help him overcome his difficulty is

(A) to discuss his difficulty with his co-workers
(B) to take the problem to the head of the organization
(C) to take the problem to the person who gave him the assignment
(D) to say nothing to anyone about his complaint

In answering this question you should study each of the choices to find which is best. Consider choice (A). Certainly an employee may discuss his complaint with fellow employees, but no change or improvement can result, and the complaint remains unsolved. Choice (B) is a poor choice since the head of the organization probably does not know what assignment you have been given, and taking your problem to him is known as "going over the head" of the supervisor. The supervisor, or person who made the assignment, is the person who can clarify it or correct any injustice. Choice (C) is, therefore, correct. To say nothing, as in choice (D), is unwise. Supervisors have an interest in knowing the problems employees are facing, and the employee is seeking a solution to his problem.

2. True-False Questions

The "true-false" or "right-wrong" form of question is sometimes used. Here a complete statement is given. Your problem is to decide whether the statement is right or wrong.

SAMPLE QUESTION:

A person-to-person long distance telephone call costs less than a station-to-station call to the same city.

This question is wrong, or "false," since person-to-person calls are more expensive.

This is not a complete list of all possible question forms, although most of the others are variations of these common types. You will always get complete directions for answering questions. Be sure you understand *how* to mark your answers -- ask questions until you do.

V. RECORDING YOUR ANSWERS

For an examination with very few applicants, you may be told to record your answers in the test booklet itself. Separate answer sheets are much more common. If this separate answer sheet is to be scored by machine -- and this is often the case -- it is highly important that you mark your answers correctly in order to get credit.

An electric test-scoring machine is often used in civil service offices because of the speed with which papers can be scored. Machine-scored answer sheets must be marked with a special pencil, which will be given to you. This pencil has a high graphite content which responds to the electrical scoring machine. As a matter of fact, stray dots may register as answers, so do not let your pencil rest on the answer sheet while you are pondering the correct answer. Also, if your pencil lead breaks or is otherwise defective, ask for another.

Since the answer sheet will be dropped in a slot in the scoring machine, be careful not to bend the corners or get the paper crumpled.

The answer sheet normally has five vertical columns of numbers, with 30 numbers to a column. These numbers correspond to the question numbers in your test booklet. After each number, going across the page, are four or five pairs of dotted lines. These short dotted lines have small letters or numbers above them. The first two pairs may also have a "T" and "F" above the letters. This indicates that the first two pairs only are to be used if the questions are of the true-false type. If the questions are multiple-choice, disregard this "T" and "F" completely, and pay attention only to the small number or letters.

Answer your questions in the manner of the sample that follows. Proceed in the sequential steps outlined below.

Assume that you are answering question 32, which is:

32. The largest city in the United States is:
   A. Washington, D.C.   B. New York City   C. Chicago
   D. Detroit   E. San Francisco

1. Choose the answer you think is best.
   New York City is the largest, so choice B is correct.
2. Find the row of dotted lines numbered the same as the question you are answering.
   This is question number 32, so find row number 32.
3. Find the pair of dotted lines corresponding to the answer you have chosen.
   You have chosen answer B, so find the pair of dotted lines marked "B".
4. Make a solid black mark between the dotted lines.
   Go up and down two or three times with your pencil so plenty of graphite rubs off, but do not let the mark get outside or above the dots.

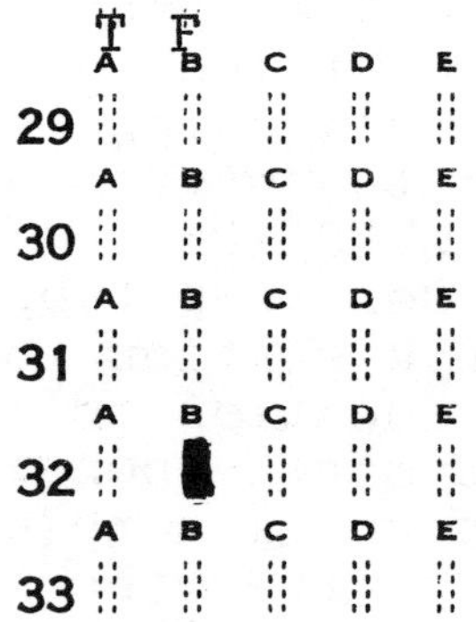

VI. BEFORE THE TEST

Common sense will help you find procedures to follow to get ready for an examination. Too many of us, however, overlook these sensible measures. Indeed, nervousness and fatigue have been found to be the most serious reasons why applicants fail to do their best on civil service tests. Here is a list of reminders.

1. Begin Your Preparation Early

Don't wait until the last minute to go scurrying around for books and materials or to find out what the position is all about.

2. Prepare Continuously

An hour a night for a week is better than an all-night cram session. This has been definitely established. What is more, a night a week for a month will return better dividends than crowding your study into a shorter period of time.

3. Locate the Place of the Examination

You have been sent a notice telling you when and where to report for the examination. If the location is in a different town or otherwise unfamiliar to you, it would be well to inquire the best route and learn something about the building.

4. Relax the Night Before the Test

Allow your mind to rest. Do not study at all that night. Plan some mild recreation or diversion; then go to bed early and get a good night's sleep.

5. Get Up Early Enough to Make a Leisurely Trip to the Place for the Test

Then unforeseen events, traffic snarls, unfamiliar buildings, will not upset you.

6. Dress Comfortably

A written test is not a fashion show. You will be known by number and not by name, so wear something comfortable.

7. Leave Excess Paraphernalia at Home

Shopping bags and odd bundles will get in your way. You need bring only the items mentioned in the official notice sent to you; usually everything you need is provided. Do not bring reference books to the examination. They will only confuse those last minutes and be taken away from you when in the test room.

8. Arrive Somewhat Ahead of Time

If because of transportation schedules you must get there very early, bring a newspaper or magazine to take your mind off yourself while waiting.

9. Locate the Examination Room

When you have found the proper room, you will be directed to the seat or part of the room where you will sit. Sometimes you are given a sheet of instructions to read while you are waiting. Do not fill out any forms until you are told to do so; just read them and be ready.

10. Relax and Prepare to Listen to the Instructions

11. If you have any physical problem that may keep you from doing your best, be sure to tell the test administrator. If you are sick, or in poor health, you really cannot do your best on the test. You can come back and take the test some other time.

VII. AT THE TEST

The day of the test is here and you have the test booklet in your hand. The temptation to get going is very strong. Caution! There is more to success than knowing the right answers. You must know how to identify your papers and understand variations in the type of short-answer question used in this particular examination. Follow these suggestions for maximum results from your efforts:

1. Cooperate with the Monitor

The test administrator has a duty to create a situation in which you can be as much at ease as possible. He will give instructions, tell you when to begin, check to see that you are marking your answer sheet correctly. He is not there to guard you, although he will see that your competitors do not take unfair advantage. He wants to help you do your best.

2. Listen to All Instructions

Don't jump the gun! Wait until you understand all directions. In most civil service tests you get more time than you need to answer the questions. So don't get in a hurry. Read each word of instructions until you clearly understand the meaning. Study the examples. Listen to all announcements. Follow directions. Ask questions if you do not understand what to do.

3. Identify Your Papers

Civil service examinations are usually identified by number only. You will be assigned a number; you must not put your name on your test papers. Be sure to copy your number correctly. Since more than one examination may be given, copy your exact examination title.

4. Plan Your Time

Unless you are told that a test is a "speed" or "rate-of-work" test, speed itself is not usually important. Time enough to answer all the questions will be provided. But this does not mean that you have all day. An overall time limit has been set. Divide the total time (in minutes) by the number of questions to get the approximate time you have for each question.

5. Do Not Linger Over Difficult Questions

If you come across a difficult question, mark it with a paper clip (useful to have along) and come back to it when you have been through the booklet. One caution if you do this -- be sure to skip a number on your answer sheet too. Check often to be sure that you have not lost your place and that you are marking in the row numbered the same as the question you are answering.

6. Read the Questions

Be sure you know what the question asks! Many capable people are unsuccessful because they failed to *read* the questions correctly.

7. Answer All Questions

Unless you have been instructed that a penalty will be deducted for incorrect answers, it is better to guess than to omit a question.

8. Speed Tests

It is often better *not* to guess on speed tests. It has been found that on timed tests people are tempted to spend the last few seconds before time is called in marking answers at random -- without even reading them -- in the hope of picking up a few extra points. To discourage this practice, the instructions may warn you that your score will be "corrected" for guessing. That is, a penalty will be applied. The incorrect answers will be deducted from the correct ones, or some other penalty formula will be used.

9. Review Your Answers

If you finish before time is called, go back to the questions you guessed or omitted to give further thought to them. Review other answers if you have time.

10. Return Your Test Materials

If you are ready to leave before others have finished or time is called, take *all* your materials to the monitor and leave quietly. Never take any test material with you. The monitor can discover whose papers are not complete, and taking a test booklet may be grounds for disqualification.

VIII. EXAMINATION TECHNIQUES

1. Read the *general* instructions carefully. These are usually printed on the first page of the examination booklet. As a rule, these instructions refer to the timing of the examination; the fact that you should not start work until the signal and must stop work at a signal, etc. If there are any *special* instructions, such as a choice of questions to be answered, make sure that you note this instruction carefully.

2. When you are ready to start work on the examination, that is as soon as the signal has been given, read the instructions to each question booklet, underline any key words or phrases, such as *least, best, outline, describe,* and the like. In this way you will tend to answer as requested rather than discover on reviewing your paper that you *listed without describing,* that you selected the *worst* choice rather than the *best* choice, etc.

3. If the examination is of the objective or so-called multiple-choice type, that is, each question will also give a series of possible answers: A, B, C, or D, and you are called upon to select the best answer and write the letter next to that answer on your answer paper, it is advisable to start answering each question in turn. There may be anywhere from 50 to 100 such questions in the three or four hours allotted and you can see how much time would be taken if you read through all the questions before beginning to answer any. Furthermore, if you come across a question or a group of questions which you know would be difficult to answer, it would undoubtedly affect your handling of all the other questions.

4. If the examination is of the esssay-type and contains but a few questions, it is a moot point as to whether you should read all the questions before starting to answer any one. Of course if you are given a choice, say five out of seven and the like, then it is essential to read all the questions so you can eliminate the two which are most difficult. If, however, you are asked to answer all the questions, there may be danger in trying to answer the easiest one first because you may find that you will spend too much time on it. The best technique is to answer the first question, then proceed to the second, etc.

5. Time your answers. Before the examination begins, write down the time it started, then add the time allowed for the examination and write down the time it must be completed, then divide the time available somewhat as follows:

(a) If 3½ hours are allowed, that would be 210 minutes. If you have 80 objective-type questions, that would be an average of 2½ minutes per question. Allow yourself no more than 2 minutes per question, or a total of 160 minutes, which will permit about 50 minutes to review.

(b) If for the time allotment of 210 minutes, there are 7 essay questions to answer, that would average about 30 minutes a question. Give yourself only 25 minutes per question so that you have about 35 minutes to review.

6. The most important instruction is *to read each question* and make sure you know what is wanted. The second most important instruction is to *time yourself properly* so that you answer every question. The third most important instruction is to *answer every question.* Guess if you have to but include something for each question. Remember that you will receive no credit for a blank and will probably receive some credit if you write something in answer to an essay question. If you guess a letter, say "B" for a multiple-choice question, you may have guessed right. If you leave a blank as the answer to a multiple-choice question, the examiners may respect your feelings but it will not add a point to your score.

7. Suggestions

a. Objective-Type Questions

(1) Examine the question booklet for proper sequence of pages and questions.
(2) Read all instructions carefully.
(3) Skip any question which seems too difficult; return to it after all other questions have been answered.
(4) Apportion your time properly; do not spend too much time on any single question or group of questions.
(5) Note and underline key words -- *all, most, fewest, least, best, worst, same, opposite.*
(6) Pay particular attention to negatives.
(7) Note unusual option, e.g., unduly long, short, complex, different or similar in content to the body of the question.
(8) Observe the use of "hedging" words -- *probably, may, most likely, etc.*
(9) Make sure that your answer is put next to the same number as the question.
(10) Do not second-guess unless you have good reason to believe the second answer is definitely more correct.
(11) Cross out original answer if you decide another answer is more accurate; do not erase.
(12) Answer all questions; guess unless instructed otherwise.
(13) Leave time for review.

b. Essay-Type Questions

(1) Read each question carefully.
(2) Determine exactly what is wanted. Underline key words or phrases.
(3) Decide on outline or paragraph answer.
(4) Include many different points and elements unless asked to develop any one or two points or elements.
(5) Show impartiality by giving pros and cons unless directed to select one side only.
(6) Make and write down any assumptions you find necessary to answer the question.
(7) Watch your English, grammar, punctuation, choice of words.
(8) Time your answers; don't crowd material.

8. Answering the Essay Question

Most essay questions can be answered by framing the specific response around several key words or ideas. Here are a few such key words or ideas:

M's: manpower, materials, methods, money, management;
P's: purpose, program, policy, plan, procedure, practice, problems, pitfalls, personnel, public relations.

a. <u>Six Basic Steps in Handling Problems</u>:
   (1) Preliminary plan and background development
   (2) Collect information, data and facts
   (3) Analyze and interpret information, data and facts
   (4) Analyze and develop solutions as well as make recommendations
   (5) Prepare report and sell recommendations
   (6) Install recommendations and follow up effectiveness

b. <u>Pitfalls to Avoid</u>
   (1) *Taking things for granted*
   A statement of the situation does not necessarily imply that each of the elements is necessarily true; for example, a complaint may be invalid and biased so that all that can be taken for granted is that a complaint has been registered.
   (2) *Considering only one side of a situation*
   Wherever possible, indicate several alternatives and then point out the reasons you selected the best one.
   (3) *Failing to indicate follow-up*
   Whenever your answer indicates action on your part, make certain that you will take proper follow-up action to see how successful your recommendations, procedures, or actions turn out to be.
   (4) *Taking too long in answering any single question*
   Remember to time your answers properly.

IX. AFTER THE TEST

Scoring procedures differ in detail among civil service jurisdictions although the general principles are the same. Whether the papers are hand-scored or graded by the electric scoring machine we have described, they are nearly always graded by number. That is, the person who marks the paper knows only the number -- never the name -- of the applicant. Not until all the papers have been graded will they be matched with names. If other tests, such as training and experience or oral interview ratings have been given, scores will be combined. Different parts of the examination usually have different weights. For example, the written test might count 60 percent of the final grade, and a rating of training and experience 40 percent. In many jurisdictions, veterans will have a certain number of points added to their grades.

After the final grade has been determined, the names are placed in grade order and an eligible list is established. There are various methods for resolving ties between those who get the same final grade: probably the most common is to place first the name of the person whose application was received first. Job offers are made from the eligible list in the order the names appear on it.

You will be notified of your grade and your rank order as soon as all these computations have been made. This will be done as rapidly as possible.

People who are found to meet the requirements in the announcement are called "eligibles." Their names are put on a list of eligibles. An eligible's chances of getting a job depend on how high he stands on this list and how fast agencies are filling jobs from the list.

When a job is to be filled from a list of eligibles, the agency asks for the names of people on the list of eligibles for that job.

When the civil service commission receives this request, it sends to the agency the names of the three people highest on the list. Or, if the job to be filled has specialized requirements, the office sends the agency, from the general list, the names of the top three persons who meet those requirements.

The appointing officer makes a choice from among the three people whose names were sent to him. If the selected person accepts the appointment, the names of the others are put back on the list to be considered for future openings.

That is the rule in hiring from all kinds of eligible lists, whether they are for typist, carpenter, chemist, or something else. For every vacancy, the appointing officer has his choice of any one of the top three eligibles on the list. This explains why the person whose name is on top of the list sometimes does not get an appointment when some of the persons lower on the list do. If the appointing officer chooses the No.2 or No.3 eligible, the No.1 eligible does not get a job at once, but stays on the list until he is appointed or the list is terminated.

X. HOW TO PASS THE INTERVIEW TEST

The examination for which you applied requires an oral interview test. You have already taken the written test and you are now being called for the interview test -- the final part of the formal examination.

You may think that it is not possible to prepare for an interview test and that there are no procedures to follow during an interview.

Our purpose is to point out some things you can do in advance that will help you and some good rules to follow and pitfalls to avoid while you are being interviewed.

A. WHAT IS AN INTERVIEW SUPPOSED TO TEST?

The written examination is designed to test the technical knowledge and competence of the candidate; the oral is designed to evaluate intangible qualities, not readily measured otherwise, and to establish a list showing the relative fitness of each candidate, *as measured against his competitors*, for the position sought. Scoring is not on the basis of "right" or "wrong," but on a sliding scale of values ranging from "not passable" to "outstanding." As a matter of fact, it is possible to achieve a relatively low score without a single "incorrect" answer because of evident weakness in the qualities being measured,

Occasionally, an examination may consist entirely of an oral test -- either an individual or a group oral. In such cases, information is sought concerning the technical knowledges and abilities of the candidate, since there has been no written examination for this purpose. More commonly, however, an oral test is used to supplement a written examination.

B. WHO CONDUCTS INTERVIEWS?

The composition of oral boards varies among different jurisdictions. In nearly all, a representative of the personnel department serves as chairman. One of the members of the board may be a representative of the department in which the candidate would work. In some cases, "outside experts" are used, and, frequently, a business man or some other representative of the general public is asked to serve. Labor and management or other special groups may be represented. The aim is to secure the services of experts in the appropriate field.

However the board is composed, it is a good idea (and not at all improper or unethical) to ascertain in advance of the interview who the members are and what groups they represent. When you are introduced to them, you will have some idea of their backgrounds and interests, and at least you will not stutter and stammer over their names.

C. WHAT TO DO BEFORE THE INTERVIEW

While knowledge about the board members is useful and takes some of the surprise element out of the interview, there is other preparation which is more substantive. It *is* possible to prepare for an oral -- in several ways:

1. <u>Keep a Copy of Your Application and Review it Carefully Before the Interview</u>

   This may be the only document before the oral board, and the starting point of the interview. Know what experience and education you have listed there, and the sequence and dates of it. Sometimes the board will ask *you* to review the highlights of your experience for them; you should not have to hem and haw doing it.

2. <u>Study the Class Specification and the Examination Announcement</u>

   Usually, the oral board has one or both of these to guide them. The qualities,characteristics,or knowledges required by the position sought are stated in these documents. They offer valuable clues as to the nature of the oral interview. For example, if the job involves supervisory responsibilities, the announcement will usually indicate that knowledge of modern supervisory methods and the qualifications of the candidate as a supervisor will be tested. If so, you can expect such questions, frequently in the form of a hypothetical situation which you are expected to solve. *Never* go into an oral without knowledge of the duties and responsibilities of the job you seek.

3. <u>Think Through Each Qualification Required</u>

   Try to visualize the kind of questions *you* would ask if you were a board member. How well could you answer them? Try especially to appraise your own knowledge and background in each area, *measured against the job sought,* and identify any areas in which you are weak. Be critical and realistic -- do not flatter yourself.

4. <u>Do Some General Reading in Areas in Which You Feel You May be Weak</u>

   For example, if the job involves supervision and your past experience has *not,* some general reading in supervisory methods and practices, particularly in the field of human relations, might be useful. *Do not* study agency procedures or detailed manuals. The oral board will be testing your understanding and capacity, *not* your memory.

5. <u>Get a Good Night's Sleep and Watch Your General Health and Mental Attitude</u>

   You will want a clear head at the interview. Take care of a cold or other minor ailment, and, of course, *no hangovers.*

D. WHAT TO DO THE DAY OF THE INTERVIEW

Now comes the day of the interview itself. Give yourself plenty of time to get there. Plan to arrive somewhat ahead of the scheduled time, particularly if your appointment is in the fore part of the day. If a previous candidate fails to appear, the board might be ready for you a bit early. By early afternoon an oral board is almost invariably behind schedule if there are many candidates, and you may have to wait. Take along a book or magazine to read, or your application to review. But leave any extraneous material in the waiting room when you go in for your interview. In any event, relax and compose yourself.

The matter of dress is important. The board is forming impressions about you -- from your experience, your manners, your attitudes, and from your appearance. Give your personal appearance careful attention. Dress your *best*, but not your flashiest. Choose conservative, appropriate clothing, and be sure it and you are immaculate. This is a business interview, and your appearance should indicate that you regard it as such. Besides, being well-groomed and properly dressed will help boost your confidence.

Sooner or later, someone will call your name and escort you into the interview room. *This is it.* From here on you are on your own. It is too late for any more preparation. But, remember, you asked for this opportunity to prove your fitness, and you are here because your request was granted.

E. WHAT HAPPENS WHEN YOU GO IN?

The usual sequence of events will be as follows: The clerk (who is often the board stenographer) will introduce you to the chairman of the oral board, who will introduce you to each other member of the board. Acknowledge the introductions before you sit down. Do not be surprised if you find a microphone facing you or a stenotypist sitting by. Oral interviews are usually recorded, in the event of an appeal or other review.

Usually the chairman of the board will open the interview by reviewing the highlights of your education and work experience from your application -- primarily for the benefit of the other members of the board, as well as to get the material into the record. Do not interrupt or comment unless there is an error or significant misinterpretation; if so, do not hesitate. But do not quibble about insignificant matters. Usually, also, he will ask you some question about your education, your experience, or your present job -- partly to get you started talking, to establish the interviewing "rapport." He may start the actual questioning, or turn it over to one of the other members. Frequently each member undertakes the questioning on a particular area, one in which he is perhaps most competent. So you can expect each member to participate in the examination. And because the time is limited, you may expect some rather abrupt switches in the direction the questioning takes. Do not be upset by it. Normally, a board member will not pursue a single line of questioning unless he discovers a particular strength or weakness.

After each member has participated, the chairman will usually ask whether any member has any further questions, then will ask you if you have anything you wish to add. Unless you are expecting this question, it may floor you. Or worse, it may start you off on an extended, extemporaneous speech. The board is not usually seeking more information. The question is principally to offer you a last opportunity to present further qualifications or to indicate that you have nothing to add. So, if you feel that a significant qualification or characteristic has been overlooked, it is proper to point it out in a sentence or so. Do not compliment the board on the thoroughness of their examination -- they have been sketchy, and you know it. If you wish, merely say, "No thank you, I have nothing further to add." This is a point where you can "talk yourself out" of a good impression or fail to present an important bit of information. *Remember, you close the interview yourself.*

The chairman will then say, "That is all, Mr. Smith, thank you." Do not be startled; the interview is over, and quicker than you think. Say, "Thank you and good morning," gather up your belongings and take your leave. Save your sigh of relief for the other side of the door.

F. HOW TO PUT YOUR BEST FOOT FORWARD

Throughout all this process, you may feel that the board individually and collectively is trying to pierce your defenses, to seek out your hidden weaknesses, and to embarrass and confuse you. Actually, this is not true. They are obliged to make an appraisal of your qualifications for the job you are seeking, and they *want to see you in your best light*. Remember, they must interview all candidates and a noncooperative candidate may become a failure in spite of their best efforts to bring out his qualifications. Here are fifteen (15) suggestions that will help you:

1. Be Natural. Keep Your Attitude Confident, But Not Cocky

If *you* are not confident that you can do the job, do not exexpect the *board* to be. Do not apologize for your weaknesses, try to bring out your strong points. The board is interested in a positive, not a negative presentation. Cockiness will antagonize any board member, and make him wonder if you are covering up a weakness by a false show of strength.

2. Get Comfortable, But Don't Lounge or Sprawl

Sit erectly but not stiffly. A careless posture may lead the board to conclude you are careless in other things, or at least that you are not impressed by the importance of the occasion to you. Either conclusion is natural, even if incorrect. Do not fuss with your clothing, or with a pencil or an ashtray. Your hands may occasionally be useful to emphasize a point; do not let them become a point of distraction.

3. Do Not Wisecrack or Make Small Talk

This is a serious situation, and your attitude should show that you consider it as such. Further, the time of the board is limited; they do not want to waste it, and neither should you.

4. Do Not Exaggerate Your Experience or Abilities

In the first place, from information in the application, from other interviews and other sources, the board may know more about you than you think; in the second place, you probably will not get away with it in the first place. An experienced board is rather adept at spotting such a situation. Do not take the chance.

5. If You Know a Member of the Board, Do Not Make a Point of It, Yet Do Not Hide It.

Certainly you are not fooling him, and probably not the other members of the board. Do not try to take advantage of your acquaintanceship -- it will probably do you little good.

6. Do Not Dominate the Interview

Let the board do that. They will give you the clues -- do not assume that you have to do all the talking. Realize that the board has a number of questions to ask you, and do not try to take up all the interview time by showing off your extensive knowledge of the answer to the first one.

7. Be Attentive

You only have twenty minutes or so, and you should keep your attention at its sharpest throughout. When a member is addressing a problem or a question to you, give him your undivided attention. Address your reply principally to him, but do not exclude the other members of the board.

8. Do Not Interrupt

A board member may be stating a problem for you to analyze. He will ask you a question when the time comes. Let him state the problem, and wait for the question.

9. Make Sure You Understand the Question

Do not try to answer until you are sure what the question is. If it is not clear, restate it in your own words or ask the board member to clarify it for you. But do not haggle about minor elements.

10. Reply Promptly But Not Hastily

A common entry on oral board rating sheets is "candidate responded readily," or "candidate hesitated in replies." Respond as promptly and quickly as you can, but do not jump to a hasty, ill-considered answer.

11. Do Not Be Peremptory in Your Answers

A brief answer is proper -- but do not fire your answer back. That is a losing game from your point of view. The board member can probably ask questions much faster than you can answer them.

12. Do Not Try To Create the Answer You Think the Board Member Wants

He is interested in what kind of mind you have and how it works -- not in playing games. Furthermore, he can usually spot this practice and will usually grade you down on it.

13. Do Not Switch Sides in Your Reply Merely to Agree With a Board Member

Frequently, a member will take a contrary position merely to draw you out and to see if you are willing and able to defend your point of view. Do not start a debate, yet do not surrender a good position. If a position is worth taking, it is worth defending.

14. Do Not Be Afraid to Admit an Error in Judgment if You Are Shown to Be Wrong

The board knows that you are forced to reply without any opportunity for careful consideration. Your answer may be demonstrably wrong. If so, admit it and get on with the interview.

15. Do Not Dwell at Length on Your Present Job

The opening question may relate to your present assignment. Answer the question but do not go into an extended discussion. You are being examined for a *new* job, not your present one. As a matter of fact, try to phrase *all* your answers in terms of the job for which you are being examined.

G. BASIS OF RATING

Probably you will forget most of these "do's" and "don'ts" when you walk into the oral interview room. Even remembering them all will not insure you a passing grade. Perhaps you did not have the qualifications in the first place. But remembering them *will* help you to put your best foot forward, without treading on the toes of the board members.

Rumor and popular opinion to the contrary notwithstanding, an oral board wants you to make the best appearance possible. They know you are under pressure -- but they also want to see how you respond to it as a guide to what your reaction would be under the pressures of the job you seek. They will be influenced by the degree of poise you display, the personal traits you show, and the manner in which you respond.

EXAMINATION SECTION

EXAMINATION SECTION

TEST 1

DIRECTIONS: Each question or incomplete statement is followed by several suggested answers or completions. Select the one that BEST answers the question or completes the statement. *PRINT THE LETTER OF THE CORRECT ANSWER IN THE SPACE AT THE RIGHT.*

1. As an expert investigator, you should realize that physical evidence gathered at a crime scene can be MOST valuable in 1.___
   A. proving identity of a suspect through circumstantial evidence
   B. proving a case against a suspect who has been previously identified
   C. proving a case against a suspect who has not been previously identified
   D. establishing the modus operandi of an unidentified criminal

2. Detectives and other investigators, in light of recent U.S. Supreme Court decisions, would be well-advised to review their investigative techniques. They should stress trying to 2.___
   A. locate evidence of guilt which is independent of confessions or admissions
   B. obtain admissions which are not connected with any physical evidence which is located
   C. obtain confessions, in writing and signed by the suspect
   D. obtain admissions and confessions which support each other

3. Certain criminals, when they engage in their chosen, illegal occupations, tend to utilize a modus operandi (M.O.) which varies little from one crime to another. It is a recommended practice to study the M.O. of various criminals because it can 3.___
   A. save time during an investigation in deciding what criminals should be questioned
   B. lead to the eventual custody of all criminals
   C. provide immediate identification of those who may have committed a crime
   D. lead to evidence which will point to those criminals dealing in illegal narcotics activity

4. Each interrogation has as its central theme one or more particular incidents of police business. All available information concerning an incident should be known to the interrogator before the interrogation is undertaken. Information concerning the incidents in question should LEAST be used as the basis for 4.___
   A. asking leading questions
   B. evaluating the information which is secured
   C. reconciling conflicting accounts of the incident
   D. stimulating a lagging interrogation

5. An investigator always makes a practice of developing an outline of the information he plans to include in a long and detailed report. Of the following, the MAIN reason for the investigator to do this additional work in the preparation of his report is to insure that the 5.___
   A. contents are accurate and factual
   B. language is technically correct and appropriate
   C. major and minor points are properly interrelated with respect to the whole
   D. length does not exceed the limitations imposed by the supervisor's available time

6. In investigating a traffic accident, an officer should question 6.___
   A. the witnesses first to find out what really happened, and then question both of the drivers at the same time to get them to agree on the facts
   B. the drivers separately, and then question the available witnesses
   C. both of the drivers at the same time, and then verify their stories by questioning the witnesses
   D. the witnesses first, and then question the drivers involved in the accident at the same time

7. As he prepares the statement being given by a witness, an investigator intentionally makes errors in the spelling of words and names. As the informant reads the statement and calls the attention of the investigator to the errors, he is offered a pen by the investigator and asked to correct the errors. 7.___
This practice is *generally*
   A. *desirable*, because the informant is made to feel that he has been very helpful to the investigator
   B. *undesirable*, because the informant will lose respect for the competence of the investigator
   C. *desirable*, because the informant cannot claim later that he did not read the statement
   D. *undesirable*, because the investigator is failing to fulfill his responsibility for the proper preparation of the statement

8. When a photographic display is used to identify a suspect, the number of photos that should be used is one of the suspect and ____ of other people. 8.___
   A. 5 B. 6 C. 7 D. 8 to 10

9. Before the viewing of a photographic display for identification purposes, the witness should be told all of the following EXCEPT 9.___
   A. to take his time and to carefully look at all the photos before making a decision
   B. that a photograph of the suspect is among the photos displayed
   C. that he should leave the photos face up
   D. that because of hair style or lighting, etc., the persons in the photos may have a different appearance than the recollection he has

10. In a line-up for identification purposes, the MINIMUM number of persons who should be used, counting the suspect, is 10.___
A. 5 B. 6 C. 7 D. 8

11. If an offender is apprehended during the preliminary investigation, police efforts during the continuing investigation should be directed toward 11.___
I. recovering stolen property
II. investigating other offenses that may have been committed by the defendant
III. developing additional leads and evidence to insure conviction

The CORRECT answer is:
A. I *only* B. I, II C. I, III D. II, III

12. During the continuing investigation, there is usually a need to perform several basic tasks. The order of these tasks may vary with the event and circumstances. 12.___
Which of the following statements regarding these tasks is INCORRECT?
A. Investigators should seek complete answers to the questions "who," "what," "when," "where," "how," and "why."
B. Theories of why and how the offense occurred should NOT be developed because such theories may direct investigators away from case solution.
C. Investigators should continue a search for new information through witnesses.
D. If evidence was submitted to the laboratory, assess the value of the reported findings.

13. With respect to "raids," which of the following statements is INCORRECT? 13.___
A. Gambling and controlled substance investigations are *usually* well-suited to a raid.
B. A raid is sometimes the ONLY effective way to bring an investigation to a successful conclusion.
C. In describing the raid plan, care should be taken NOT to disclose the location of the raid since there may be a leak in security.
D. Cover groups to block escape routes should be deployed in advance of the raiding party's invasion.

14. Basic to all police reports but of special importance to complaint investigation reports are the requisites of accuracy and completeness. 14.___
The CORRECT statement(s) regarding the above statement is(are):
I. Investigators should NOT include their opinions in reports unless requested to do so by their superior
II. Proper names should be used in the report rather than such terms as "suspect," "arrestee," etc.
III. Recommendations by the investigator should never be included in the report.

The CORRECT answer is:
A. I *only* B. I, II C. I, III D. II, III
E. III *only*

15. The preliminary investigation is usually, but not always, performed by uniformed officers on patrol because 15.____
I. quick response may result in immediate apprehension of the offender
II. a uniformed officer is BEST able to go to the scene quickly
III. at the scene, a uniformed officer is better able to control the situation and to get information quickly
The statement is supported by reasons
A. I B. I, II C. I, II, III D. II, III

16. With respect to the investigation of unattended deaths, which of the following statements is INCORRECT? 16.____
A. They should all be treated as homicides until proven otherwise.
B. The first officer to arrive at any possible homicide scene should immediately record the date, time, location, and weather conditions.
C. All persons, including police officers, who do not have an official function to perform should be excluded from a possible homicide scene.
D. The investigator must be able to establish a motive since no conviction is possible without one.

17. Which of the following statements is INCORRECT? 17.____
A. If you wish to intercept ransom mail addressed to the victim's family, get written authorization from them.
B. Before any ransom demand is met, the kidnapper should be requested to supply information known only to the family and the victim.
C. You should advise the family whether or not to respond to the ransom demand.
D. If the ransom is to be paid and the money photographed, permission should be obtained from the U.S. Secret Service.

18. The investigation of obscenity offenses often presents difficult problems to the police investigator. 18.____
The LEAST CORRECT statement is:
A. The investigating officer should confer with the District Attorney in ALL obscenity offenses.
B. Under the guidelines of the Supreme Court, an investigating officer may make a determination that something is obscene and consequently may take certain kinds of immediate enforcement action.
C. The investigating officer should have a judge or the district attorney view the items or obscene acts prior to making an arrest.
D. A search warrant cannot be obtained unless the application describes the specific items to be seized.

19. The State issues licenses or registers and regulates some thirty separate categories of professionals that practice in the State. 19.___
The INCORRECT statement concerning investigative suggestions is:
A. Police officers may be involved in the investigation of unauthorized acts by these professionals, but investigations concerning professional misconduct should be conducted by special investigators employed by the State.
B. A police officer should NOT begin an investigation or make a summary arrest of a professional person for an unauthorized act in violation of the Education Law without first conferring with a supervising officer regarding the facts of the alleged unauthorized act.
C. If requested by the District Attorney, a police officer should notify the proper State agency of any unauthorized acts performed by a professional person.
D. When a police officer receives a complaint of professional misconduct, he should instruct the complainant to seek the assistance of special investigators employed by the State to look into the matter.

20. Which of the following is NOT a properly stated investigative suggestion when an officer has reason to believe that illegal gambling activity is occurring in his patrol area? 20.___
A. Attempt to ascertain the type (horse, sports, numbers, cards, etc.) of gambling being conducted.
B. Attempt to ascertain the location where "action" is taken.
C. Attempt to ascertain some indication of the daily amount bet.
D. After gathering information, the patrol officer should report such to the vice detail supervisor verbally to preserve the security and integrity of the information.

KEY (CORRECT ANSWERS)

1. B	11. B
2. A	12. B
3. A	13. C
4. A	14. B
5. C	15. C
6. B	16. D
7. C	17. C
8. D	18. B
9. B	19. B
10. B	20. D

TEST 2

Questions 1 to 13.

DIRECTIONS: Each question or incomplete statement is followed by several suggested answers or completions. Select the one that BEST answers the question or completes the statement. *PRINT THE LETTER OF THE CORRECT ANSWER IN THE SPACE AT THE RIGHT.*

1. The INCORRECT statement regarding investigative suggestions concerning refusing to aid a peace officer or a police officer is: 1.___
   A. If applicable, the officer concerned should identify and interview witnesses and obtain depositions.
   B. The evidence must clearly establish that an understandable request or command was given.
   C. Failure to comply with an unreasonable command by a peace officer or police officer is NOT a violation of refusing to aid a peace officer or a police officer.
   D. The defined term "reasonableness" as it appears in the Penal Law must be used to determine if the request was reasonable or not.

2. Which of the following is NOT a properly stated investigative suggestion in sex crime cases? 2.___
   A. Interview and obtain detailed statements from the complainant, the victim, and any witnesses.
   B. Emphasis must be placed on using the victim's and witnesses' own words in the statements.
   C. If the victim is under 18 years old, consider having a parent or guardian present at the time the interview is conducted and when the statement is taken.
   D. If a child is the victim, notify the parents immediately.

3. The INCORRECT statement regarding investigative suggestions in bribery cases is: 3.___
   A. Officers should take signed statements in all bribery related cases. These statements should set forth the details of the crime, including the exact words used during the transaction.
   B. In ALL instances where a complaint is received before the bribery has been completed, a planned payoff under police surveillance should be considered.
   C. Electronic technical surveillance should be considered regarding phone conversations, either under court order or with the written consent of one of the parties to the conversation or telephone calls.
   D. Officers should confer with their commanding officer regarding the obtaining of the appropriate search warrants or subpoenas.

4. Which of the following statements is not consistent with the Alcoholic Beverage Control Law? 4.____
   A. "Alcoholic beverage" or "beverage" mean and include alcohol, spirits, liquor, wine, beer, cider, and every liquid or solid, patented or not, containing alcohol, spirits, wine or beer and capable of being consumed by a human being, and any warehouse receipt, certificate, contract or other document pertaining thereto.
   B. "Convicted" and "conviction" include and mean a finding of guilt resulting from a plea of guilty, the decision of a court or magistrate or the verdict of a jury, irrespective of the pronouncement of judgment or the suspension thereof.
   C. "Drug store" means a place registered by the State Board of Pharmacy for the sale of prescription and non-prescription medicines excluding the sale of drugs.
   D. "Retail sale" or "sale at retail" means a sale to a consumer or to any person for any purpose other than for resale.

5. No person shall sell, deliver or give away or cause or permit or procure to be sold, delivered or given away any alcoholic beverages to any 5.____
   I. person actually or apparently under the age of 20 years
   II. intoxicated person or to any person, actually or apparently under the influence of liquor
   III. habitual drunkard known to be such to the person authorized to dispense any alcoholic beverages

   The CORRECT answer is:
   A. I B. I, II C. I, II, III D. II, III

6. Fingerprints are required to be taken when an arrest is made for a non-penal law misdemeanor that would become a felony based on a previous conviction. Perhaps the most familiar of these is D.W.I. (1192 V.T.L.). Some less familiar situations exist in the law. 6.____
   Consider the following and decide whether or not a prior conviction(s) would make the crime a felony.
   I. 152 A.B.C. Law (sale of illicit alcohol)
   II. 481 Tax Law (sale, etc. of unstamped cigarettes)
   III. 392a V.T.L. (sale of false or fraudulent license, registration, or number plate)
   IV. Article 17 of Election Law (violations of elective franchise)

   The crimes that would become felonies are:
   A. I, II B. II, IV
   C. III, IV D. I, II, III, IV

7. John Simons, an 18-year-old male, entered O'Grady's Bar & Grill and ordered a scotch and soda. The bartender, Steven Hall, was suspicious about the age of Simons. Simons then produced a photographic identification card from a government institution which indicated that he, Simons, was 21 years of age. Hall then served the drink to John Simons. 7.____

According to the above paragraph, the CORRECT statement(s) is(are):

I. In any subsequent proceeding which might arise from the "sale to someone under the age of 21 years," Steven Hall would have an affirmative defense in that John Simons had produced the phony identification as described above.

II. No person refusing to serve someone an alcoholic beverage whom he believes to be actually or apparently under 21 years of age shall be liable in ANY civil or criminal action or for any fine or penalty based on such refusal.

The CORRECT answer is:

A. I
B. II
C. both of the above
D. neither of the above

8. The INCORRECT statement regarding the Alcoholic Beverage Control law is: 8.___

A. Any person who misrepresents the age of a person under the age of 19 years for the purpose of inducing the sale of any alcoholic beverage is guilty of an offense and upon conviction thereof shall be punished by a fine of not more than $200, or by imprisonment for not more than five days, or by both such fine and imprisonment.
B. Any person under the age of 19 years who presents or offers to any licensee under the Alcoholic Beverage Control law, or to an employee of such licensee, any written evidence which is false, etc.... or not actually his own, for the purpose of purchasing or attempting to purchase, any alcoholic beverages, may be arrested or summoned and be examined by a magistrate... on a charge of illegally purchasing or attempting to illegally purchase an alcoholic beverage.
C. Regarding B above, if a determination is made sustaining such charge, the court or magistrate shall release such person on probation for a period of not exceeding one year, and MAY, in addition, impose a fine not exceeding $100.
D. A determination as described in C above shall be deemed a conviction.

9. Evaluate the following statements regarding the Alcoholic Beverage Control law: 9.___

I. No retailer shall employ on any premises licensed for retail sale, any person under the age of 18 years, as a hostess, waitress, waiter, or in any other capacity where the duties of such person require or permit such person to sell, dispense or handle alcoholic beverages with certain exceptions.

II. Any person under 18 years and employed by any person holding a grocery store beer license shall be permitted to handle and deliver beer for such licensee.

III. Any person under the age of 18 years of age employed as a cashier by a person holding a grocery store beer license shall be permitted to record and receive payment for beer sales when in the presence of and under the direct supervision of a person 18 years of age or over.

The CORRECT answer is:
A. All of the statements are accurate
B. Only A and B are accurate
C. Only B and C are accurate
D. None of the statements is accurate

10. Select the incorrect statement according to the Alcoholic Beverage Control law. No premises licensed to sell liquor and/or wine for off-premises consumption shall be permitted to remain open: 10.___
A. On Sunday
B. On any other day between 10 P.M. and 8 A.M.
C. On the 25th day of December, known as Christmas Day, and if any such day is Sunday, the next day thereafter
D. In any community where daylight savings time is in effect, such time shall be deemed the standard time for purpose of this law

11. Of the following, the INCORRECT statement is: 11.___
A. A prisoner conveyed to jail through another county by a sheriff or other officer pursuant to law, or the officer having him in custody, is NOT liable to arrest in any civil action or special proceeding, while passing through another county.
B. A person duly and in good faith subpoenaed or ordered to attend, for the purpose of being examined, in a case where his attendance may lawfully be enforced is privileged from arrest in a civil action or special proceeding while going to, remaining at, and returning from, the place where he is required to attend.
C. All personnel records used to evaluate performance, etc. under the control of any police agency or department of the state shall be considered confidential and NOT subject to inspection or review without the express written consent of such police officer (or correction officer) except as may be mandated by lawful court order.
D. The identity of any victim of a sex offense shall be confidential.

12. The CORRECT statement(s) regarding problem drinking is(are): 12.___
I. Alcohol dependence is the most serious drug problem in the country.
II. A drinking problem may exist without the person being aware of it.
III. When problem drinking causes the employee's job performance to deteriorate or results in misconduct that justifies negative disciplinary action, the supervisor is obligated to take action.

The CORRECT answer is:
A. I, II
B. I, II, III
C. II, III
D. None of the above

13. The INCORRECT statement regarding alcoholism is: 13.___
A. The alcoholic doesn't have to hit bottom before realizing he needs help.
B. Disciplining a subordinate for problem drinking is not compatible with treatment.
C. There are times when a supervisor may be obligated to take negative disciplinary action.
D. Telling a problem drinker that he has the problem may not be proper.

DIRECTIONS: Each question consists of a statement. You are to indicate whether the statement is TRUE (T) or FALSE (F). *PRINT THE LETTER OF THE CORRECT ANSWER IN THE SPACE AT THE RIGHT.*

Questions 14-15.

Indicate whether the following statements in Questions 14-15 are true or false regarding investigative suggestions for unlawfully dealing with fireworks and creating a hazard.

14. The officer concerned should check to ascertain if a permit was obtained from the proper authority for a public display of fireworks. 14.___

15. In these fireworks cases, defendants should be interviewed to determine the source of supply and the possible involvement of other persons. 15.___

Questions 16-20.

Indicate whether the following statements in Questions 16-20 are true or false regarding investigative suggestions in sex crimes.

16. Have the victim examined by a physician *immediately* to obtain evidence of the crime and to provide any necessary medical treatment. 16.___

17. Color photographs of the victim's injuries should be taken in conjunction with any medical examination. 17.___

18. In ALL cases, conduct neighborhood interviews. 18.___

19. Consider requesting the state police laboratory to supply a psychological profile of the offender. 19.___

20. Conduct a background investigation of all suspects. 20.___

KEY (CORRECT ANSWERS)

1.	D	11.	D
2.	C	12.	B
3.	D	13.	B
4.	C	14.	T
5.	D	15.	T
6.	D	16.	T
7.	C	17.	T
8.	D	18.	F
9.	A	19.	F
10.	B	20.	T

EXAMINATION SECTION

TEST 1

DIRECTIONS: Each question or incomplete statement is followed by several suggested answers or completions. Select the one that BEST answers the question or completes the statement. *PRINT THE LETTER OF THE CORRECT ANSWER IN THE SPACE AT THE RIGHT.*

1. Assume that you are interviewing a witness who is telling a story crucial to your investigation. It is important that you get all the facts being related by this witness. In order to secure this vital information, the BEST of the following techniques is to 1.____
   A. quietly interrupt the witness's story and request him to speak with deliberation so that you can record his statement
   B. guide the witness during his recital so that all important points are validated
   C. confine your activities during the story to brief note-taking; and after the information has been secured, request a full written statement
   D. inform the witness that he must relate all the facts as truthfully and concisely as possible

2. The statement of any witness obtained by an investigator in an interview should GENERALLY be considered 2.____
   A. as a lead requiring substantiation by additional evidence
   B. accurate if the witness appears honest and is cooperative
   C. unreliable if the witness has been involved in similar investigations
   D. as a fact admissible under the rules of evidence

3. During an important interview, an investigator takes notes from time to time but very rarely looks at the subject being questioned. 3.____
   Such action on the part of the investigator is
   A. *unacceptable*, chiefly because during the actual interview an investigator should pay more attention to the witness's manner of giving the information rather than to the content of his statement
   B. *acceptable*, chiefly because data should be recorded at the earliest opportunity and important data should be noted meticulously
   C. *unacceptable*, chiefly because it inhibits the person being interviewed and is not conducive to a give-and-take discussion
   D. *acceptable*, chiefly because focusing attention on note-taking and not on the person being interviewed creates an impression of professional objectivity

4. The BEST source with which to check the credit rating of a business you are investigating is 4.____
   A. the Better Business Bureau
   B. Standard and Poor's
   C. Dun and Bradstreet, Inc.
   D. the State Attorney General's Office

5. Since he must, in the course of his investigations, interview persons with various personalities and attitudes, an investigator should GENERALLY adopt a method of interviewing that 5.____
   A. is uniformly applicable to all types so that discrepancies in the accounts of individuals may be readily detected
   B. can be adjusted to the persons whom he interviews
   C. is based on the premise that most witnesses tend to be uncooperative
   D. requires the investigator to spend as little time as possible in questioning witnesses

6. An investigator finds that X, Y, and Z are eyewitnesses to an incident under investigation. He interviews X, who gives him a complete and very detailed statement about the incident. X also informs the investigator that he has discussed the matter with Y and Z, and that each of them completely agrees with him as to what had occurred. 6.____
   Under these circumstances, it would be MOST appropriate for the investigator to
   A. interview Y and Z before assessing the value of the statements made by the three witnesses
   B. interview Y and Z and accept their versions if they both disagree with the story given by witness X
   C. interview either Y or Z and close the investigation if the statement of either witness agrees with the story given by witness X
   D. close the investigation on the basis of his interview with witness X since there is no reason to assume that Y and Z will tell a different story

7. Which one of the following is a legal requirement for the admissibility of evidence in a legal proceeding? 7.____
   A. Weight
   B. Sufficiency
   C. Competency
   D. Recency

8. Of the following diagrams, which one represents the CORRECT utilization of the ABC Method of Surveillance? 8.____
Note: S - identifies the suspect's position
X - identifies the positions of investigators
Arrow indicates direction in which suspect is moving

A.

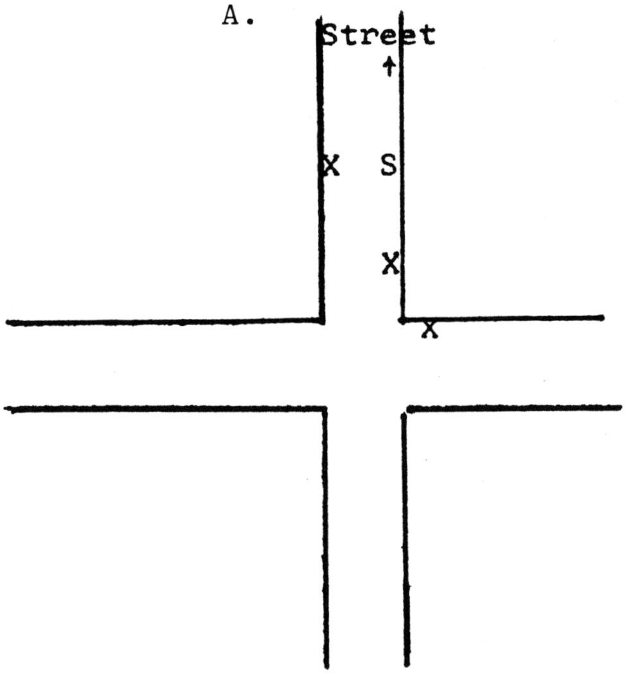

B.

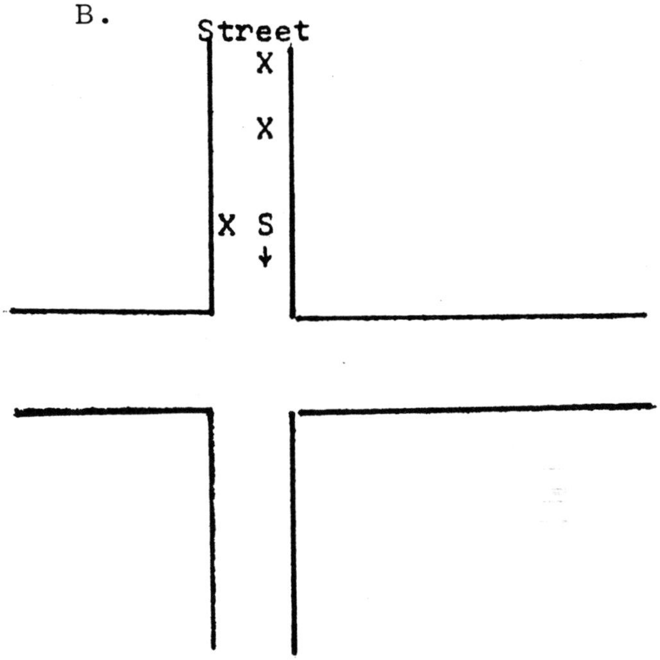

C.

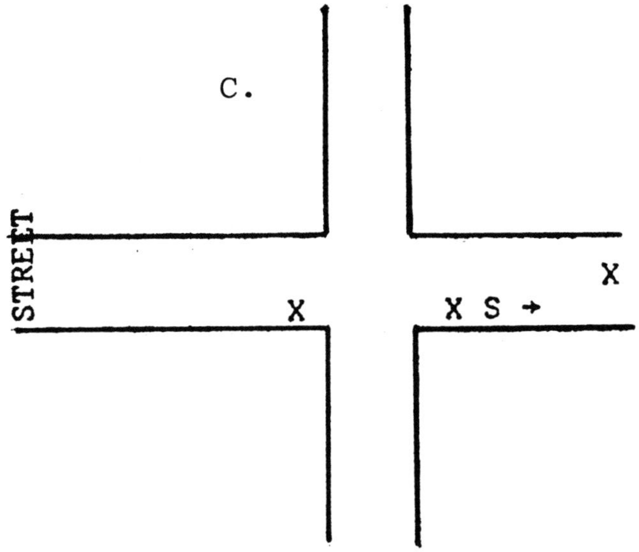

D.

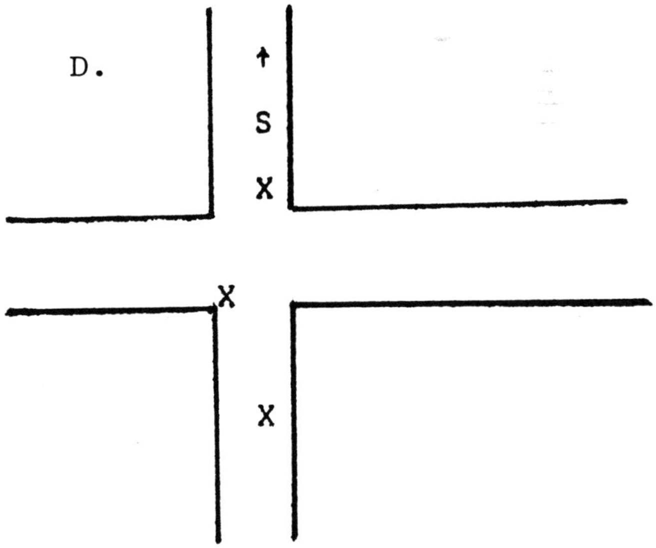

9. During an interview, an interviewee makes the following statement: *I have given the problem of getting a job a great deal of thought. I am looking primarily for an opportunity to grow and develop - to find the type of job that will provide the greatest challenge and bring out the best that is in me. Security probably ranks at the bottom of my list since I feel that I can always make a living somewhere.* 9.____
From an analysis of this statement, an investigator would be LEAST likely to conclude that the interviewee is
   A. capable of analytical thought
   B. looking for job satisfaction
   C. seeking self-improvement
   D. trying to cover for his lack of self-confidence

10. One of the more difficult tasks facing an investigator in an interview is to control the tendency of witnesses to ramble when giving information. 10.____
Of the following, the BEST technique for keeping a witness's comments pertinent is to
   A. ask questions which indicate the desired answer
   B. insist on *yes* and *no* answers to his questions
   C. construct questions that restrict the range of information which the witness can give in response
   D. ask precise questions so that the answers of the witness will necessarily be brief

11. The BASIC purpose of producing evidence in legal proceedings is to 11.____
   A. provide a permanent official record for legal action
   B. screen out confusing issues of law and fact
   C. determine the truth of a matter in issue
   D. insure that hearsay statements will be excluded

12. An investigator is handling a case involving an individual and finds that the case is proving very difficult because he has run out of leads to follow up. 12.____
Of the following, the BEST way for the investigator to deal with this case is FIRST to
   A. prepare a report of the case indicating that no further action can be taken
   B. place himself in the position of the person being investigated
   C. re-interview all those affected by the case until a new clue is revealed
   D. wait for the first break in the case which will give a substantial lead

13. Assume that you need to interview a person who is suspected of collaborating with the subject under investigation. 13.____
Of the following, the interviewing procedure that is MOST appropriate for handling this situation is to

A. conduct a casual interview with the person on a pretext different from the actual purpose of the interview
B. interview the person intensively by means of the *team* method until he breaks down and gives information
C. insist that the suspected person cooperate
D. plan to review every statement made by the person until he realizes that no fact will be overlooked

14. Assume that two disinterested individuals had directly witnessed the same event. An investigator who interviewed them received two distinctly different versions of this event. 14.____
Which of the following assumptions PROBABLY accounts for the difference in the two versions?
A. The event must have consisted of so many separate happenings that no one could understand everything that occurred.
B. Each individual was selective in his perception of the event.
C. The interviewing technique used by the investigator was instrumental in eliciting different facts from each individual.
D. One of the individuals wishes to cooperate with the investigator, but the other did not.

15. During interviews, a certain investigator phrases follow-up questions mentally during pauses while the subject is still answering the previous question. 15.____
This practice is GENERALLY
A. *desirable*, chiefly because it gives the impression that the investigator is well-acquainted with all the facts
B. *undesirable*, chiefly because the investigator cannot know whether such questions will be appropriate
C. *desirable*, chiefly because it enables the investigator to pose new questions without significant breaks in the discussion
D. *undesirable*, chiefly because it subjects the person being interviewed to a barrage of questions

16. Generally, a professional investigator's practice of training himself to give the impression of telling the truth during court appearances is considered 16.____
A. *desirable*, chiefly because only by such practice can he perfect his ability to give accurate testimony
B. *undesirable*, chiefly because any deviation from the unadulterated truth by using a pretension constitutes perjury
C. *desirable*, chiefly because such training lessens the possibility of his appearing nervous and timid while testifying, which might convey the impression that he is evasive or lying

D. *undesirable*, chiefly because all testimony should be given in a natural manner, including hesitations, to avoid the court's suspicion that the witness has been coached

17. Assume that prior to an interview, a person makes a spontaneous declaration relating to his case in the presence of an investigator. 17.___
According to a rule of evidence, the person's statement is GENERALLY
A. *admissible*, only if the investigator testifies to the declaration and his testimony is corroborated by another person
B. *inadmissible*, chiefly because it constitutes a hearsay declaration against the person's interest
C. *admissible*, chiefly because it was not the product of the person's deliberation and reflection
D. *inadmissible*, chiefly because the person was under duress when the exclamation was made

18. In order to break down the communication barriers between an interviewer and his subject, the interviewer should GENERALLY ask introductory questions which 18.___
A. focus on the individual's job status
B. can be answered in a *yes-or-no* fashion
C. focus directly on official business
D. are likely to be of mutual interest to the two parties

19. To introduce as evidence a set of business books prepared by a person other than the individual under investigation, preliminary evidence pertaining to the content of the books must first be established. 19.___
Which of the following does NOT constitute a fact which must be established before such books may be admitted as evidence?
The
A. entries were made in the regular course of business at or about the time of the transactions involved
B. books have been audited and certified as correct
C. books are the regular books used for making business entries
D. entries in the books were made by persons required to make them in the course of their regular duties

20. A person who is suffering from a mental disability is not necessarily disqualified from testifying as a witness in a legal proceeding PROVIDED that such person 20.___
A. has the ability to recall and describe past events pertaining to the case
B. is not an inmate of a mental institution
C. is attended by a qualified psychiatrist at all times while in the courtroom
D. swears that he knows the difference between right and wrong

21. Of the following public records, which is the BEST single source of information on the personal history and background of a subject? 21.____
   A. Birth or baptismal certificate
   B. Marriage license application
   C. Discharge certificate from the military services
   D. Income tax return

22. When it is necessary to prove the contents of a written instrument concerning a matter in dispute, the *best evidence rule* provides that 22.____
   A. the contents of written instruments must be subscribed and sworn to before a notary public to be admissible in legal proceedings
   B. no evidence outside the instrument itself shall be used to alter the wording of the instrument
   C. a witness who qualifies as an expert in handwriting identification shall first testify on the genuineness of the instrument
   D. the original instrument itself must be produced in court if it is available

23. Public documents, if otherwise competent, are admissible as evidence of the facts recorded therein, without the testimony of the officers who entered the facts, CHIEFLY because 23.____
   A. public records are subject to such strict security that the entries therein cannot be altered or falsified
   B. all such documents require further corroboration before they are admissible as proof of any facts recorded therein
   C. entries in these documents are made by officers who have sworn to perform their duties in the public interest
   D. hearsay evidence may not be admitted to prove a fact in dispute without the testimony of the officer who recorded it

24. One of the following ways in which an investigator might ordinarily detect an inconsistency in an interviewee's story is by 24.____
   A. having a third party present during the interview
   B. requesting the subject to speak more slowly
   C. observing the subject's manner of dress or attire
   D. watching the subject's facial expressions and mannerisms

25. The use of small talk or conversation about extraneous topics such as sports, the weather, or current events at the start of a routine interview designed to elicit information is GENERALLY considered 25.____
   A. *desirable*, chiefly because it gives the subject a chance to relax and relieve himself of the tension that normally develops before an interview

B. *undesirable*, chiefly because it wastes the valuable time of subjects with matters that are unrelated to the purpose of the interview
C. *desirable*, chiefly because it is the only way the interviewer is able to ascertain whether he and the subject will be able to develop rapport
D. *undesirable*, chiefly because it is possible to obtain more information about the subject if he is unaware of the purpose of the interview

26. Assume that your superior assigns you to interview an individual who, he warns, seems to be highly *introverted*. You should be aware that, during an interview, such a person is likely to 26.___
A. hold views which are highly controversial in nature
B. be domineering and try to control the direction of the interview
C. resist answering personal questions regarding his background
D. give information which is largely fabricated

27. The one of the following persons who is MOST likely to be willing to give information leading to the apprehension of a suspect is someone who is 27.___
A. friendly with the suspect
B. afraid of the suspect
C. interested in law enforcement
D. seeking revenge against the suspect

28. During the course of a routine interview, the BEST tone of voice for an interviewer to use is 28.___
A. authoritative B. uncertain
C. formal D. conversational

29. It is recommended that interviews which inquire into the personal background of an individual should be held in private. 29.___
The BEST reason for this practice is that privacy
A. allows the individual to talk freely about the details of his background
B. induces contemplative thought on the part of the interviewed individual
C. prevents any interruptions by departmental personnel during the interview
D. most closely resembles the atmosphere of the individual's personal life

30. Of the following, the MOST preferable way for an investigator to make a reference check on a subject's previous employment in the area is to 30.___
A. write to the employer and ask him to fill out a standard employee evaluation form
B. call the employer and conduct a telephone interview
C. write to the employer and request a personal interview
D. telephone the employer and ask him to submit a written evaluation

31. Of the following, the BEST way for an investigator to prepare himself for a court appearance as a witness is generally by 31.____
   A. memorizing every detail of the case in order to give an exact recital of the information
   B. reviewing his notes and trying to fix in his mind the highlights of the case
   C. consulting with his superiors in order to ascertain which aspects of the case should be emphasized
   D. studying all aspects of the case and writing out in detail the testimony he intends to give under oath

32. When an investigator is called as a witness to relate a series of incidents, his testimony should GENERALLY consist of 32.____
   A. a background narrative, followed by important facts and a concluding statement
   B. important facts, followed by a background narrative and a concluding statement
   C. details personally observed followed by any undeveloped leads
   D. a simple chronological account of the events he has observed

33. Of the following, an individual who smokes heavily during interrogation or an interview is LEAST likely to experience a(n) 33.____
   A. decrease in mental efficiency
   B. decrease in physical efficiency
   C. state of high emotion during questioning
   D. emotional release during questioning

34. The BEST way for an investigator to handle a situation in which the person interviewed asks a few slightly personal questions is generally to 34.____
   A. give quick, evasive answers and continue with the interview
   B. tell the person such questions are irrelevant and objectionable
   C. inquire fully into the person's reasons for wanting such information
   D. answer the questions briefly and truthfully

35. The CHIEF purpose of using surveillance in an investigation is to 35.____
   A. obtain information about persons and activities
   B. cause suspected persons to feel continuously uneasy
   C. maintain a close watch over hostile witnesses
   D. induce subjects to volunteer information

36. A *surreptitious* recording of an interview is one which is made 36.____
   A. whenever the information is highly technical
   B. to conceal the identity of the interviewee
   C. without the knowledge of the subject
   D. to encourage a subject to be more informative

37. All the means by which any alleged matter of fact, the truth of which is submitted to investigation, is established or disproved is the legal definition of 37.____
A. proof
B. burden of proof
C. evidence
D. admissibility of evidence

38. That section of an affidavit in which an officer empowered to administer an oath certifies that this document was *sworn to* before him is called a(n) 38.____
A. affirmation
B. jurat
C. acknowledgement
D. verification

39. In legal terminology, a *bailee* is a person who 39.____
A. lawfully holds property belonging to another
B. deposits cash or property for the release of an arrested person
C. has been released from arrest on a bond that guarantees his court appearance
D. deposits personal property as collateral for a debt

40. A specimen of handwriting of known authorship which can be used by an investigator for making a comparison with a questioned or suspected writing is called a(n) 40.____
A. inscription
B. precis
C. coordinate
D. exemplar

41. The attorney felt that his client would be *exonerated*. 41.____
In this sentence, *exonerated* means MOST NEARLY
A. unwilling to testify
B. declared blameless
C. severely punished
D. placed on probation

42. The two witnesses were suspected of *collusion*. 42.____
In this sentence, the word *collusion* means MOST NEARLY
A. a conflict of interest
B. an unintentional error
C. an illegal secret agreement
D. financial irregularities

43. Many of the subject's answers during the interview were *redundant*. 43.____
In this sentence, *redundant* means MOST NEARLY
A. uninformative
B. thoughtful
C. repetitious
D. argumentative

44. He was assigned to investigate an individual who was *insolvent*. 44.____
In this sentence, *insolvent* means MOST NEARLY
A. unable to pay debts
B. extremely disrespectful
C. difficult to understand
D. frequently out of work

45. In his report, the investigator described several *covert* business transactions. 45.____
In this sentence, *covert* means MOST NEARLY
A. unauthorized
B. joint
C. complicated
D. secret

KEY (CORRECT ANSWERS)

1. C	10. C	19. B	28. D	37. C
2. A	11. C	20. A	29. A	38. B
3. C	12. B	21. B	30. A	39. A
4. C	13. A	22. D	31. B	40. D
5. B	14. B	23. C	32. D	41. B
6. A	15. C	24. D	33. C	42. C
7. C	16. C	25. A	34. D	43. C
8. C	17. C	26. C	35. A	44. A
9. D	18. D	27. D	36. C	45. D

TEST 2

DIRECTIONS: Each question or incomplete statement is followed by several suggested answers or completions. Select the one that BEST answers the question or completes the statement. *PRINT THE LETTER OF THE CORRECT ANSWER IN THE SPACE AT THE RIGHT.*

Questions 1-5.

DIRECTIONS: Questions 1 through 5 consist of two sentences which may or may not contain errors in word usage or sentence structure, punctuation, or capitalization. Consider a sentence correct although there may be other correct ways of expressing the same thought.
Mark your answer:
A. If only Sentence I is correct;
B. If only Sentence II is correct;
C. If Sentences I and II are both correct;
D. If Sentences I and II are both incorrect.

1. I. Being locked in his desk, the investigator felt sure that the records would be safe. 1.____
II. The reason why the witness changed his statement was because he had been threatened.

2. I. The investigation had just began then an important witness disappeared. 2.____
II. The check that had been missing was located and returned to its owner, Harry Morgan, a resident of Suffolk County, New York.

3. I. A supervisor will find that the establishment of standard procedures enables his staff to work more efficiently. 3.____
II. An investigator hadn't ought to give any recommendations in his report if he is in doubt.

4. I. Neither the investigator nor his supervisor is ready to interview the witnesses. 4.____
II. Interviewing has been and always will be an important asset in investigation.

5. I. One of the investigator's reports has been forwarded to the wrong person. 5.____
II. The investigator stated that he was not familiar with those kind of cases.

Questions 6-8.

DIRECTIONS: Questions 6 through 8 are to be answered SOLELY on the basis of the following passage.

As investigators, we are more concerned with the utilitarian than the philosophical aspects of ethics and ethical standards, procedures, and conduct. As a working consideration, we might view ethics as the science of doing the right thing at the right time in the right manner in conformity with the normal, everyday standards imposed by society; and in conformity with the judgment society would be expected to make concerning the rightness or wrongness of what we have done.

An ethical code might be considered a basic set of rules and regulations to which we must conform in the performance of investigative duties. Ethical standards, procedures, and conduct might be considered the logical workings of our ethical code in its everyday application to our work. Ethics also necessarily involves morals and morality. We must eventually answer the self-imposed question of whether or not we have acted in the right way in conducting our investigative activities in their individual and total aspects.

6. Of the following, the MOST suitable title for the above passage is 6.____
   A. THE IMPORTANCE OF RULES FOR INVESTIGATORS
   B. THE BASIC PHILOSOPHY OF A LAWFUL SOCIETY
   C. SCIENTIFIC ASPECTS OF INVESTIGATIONS
   D. ETHICAL GUIDELINES FOR THE CONDUCT OF INVESTIGATIONS

7. According to the above passage, ethical considerations for investigators involve 7.____
   A. special standards that are different from those which apply to the rest of society
   B. practices and procedures which cannot be evaluated by others
   C. individual judgments by investigators of the appropriateness of their own actions
   D. regulations which are based primarily upon a philosophical approach

8. Of the following, the author's PRINCIPAL purpose in writing the above passage seems to have been to 8.____
   A. emphasize the importance of self-criticism in investigative activities
   B. explain the relationship that exists between ethics and investigative conduct
   C. reduce the amount of unethical conduct in the area of investigations
   D. seek recognition by his fellow investigators for his academic treatment of the subject matter

Questions 9-11.

DIRECTIONS: Questions 9 through 11 are to be answered SOLELY on the basis of the following passage.

The investigator must remember that acts of omission can be as effective as acts of commission in affecting the determination of disputed issues. Acts of omission, such as failure to obtain available information or failure to verify dubious information, manifest themselves in miscarriages of justice and erroneous adjudications. An incomplete investigation is an erroneous investigation because a conclusion predicated upon inadequate facts is based on quicksand.

When an investigator throws up his hands and admits defeat, the reason for this action does not necessarily lie in his possible laziness and ineptitude. It is more likely that the investigator has made his conclusions after exhausting only those avenues of investigation of which he is aware. He has exercised good faith in his belief that nothing else can be done.

This tendency must be overcome by all investigators if they are to operate at top efficiency. If no suggestion for new or additional action can be found in any authority, an investigator should use his own initiative to cope with a given situation. No investigator should ever hesitate to set precedents. It is far better in the final analysis to attempt difficult solutions, even if the chances of error are obviously present, than it is to take refuge in the spinless adage: If you don't do anything, you don't do it wrong.

9. Of the following, the MOST suitable title for the above passage is 9.____
   A. THE NEED FOR RESOURCEFULNESS IN INVESTIGATIONS
   B. PROCEDURES FOR COMPLETING AN INVESTIGATION
   C. THE DEVELOPMENT OF STANDARDS FOR INVESTIGATORS
   D. THE CAUSES OF INCOMPLETE INVESTIGATIONS

10. Of the following, the author of this passage considers that the LEAST important consideration in developing new investigative methods is 10.____
   A. efficiency
   B. caution
   C. imagination
   D. thoroughness

11. According to this passage, which of the following statements is INCORRECT? 11.____
   A. Lack of creativity may lead to erroneous investigations.
   B. Acts of omission are sometimes as harmful as acts of commission.
   C. Some investigators who give up on a case are lazy or inept.
   D. An investigator who gives up on a case is usually not acting in good faith.

Questions 12-15.

DIRECTIONS: Questions 12 through 15 are to be answered SOLELY on the basis of the following passage.

Perpetrators of crimes are often described by witnesses or victims in terms of salient facial features. The Bertillon System of Identification, which preceded the widespread use of fingerprints, was based on body measurements. Recently, there have been developments in the quantification of procedures used in the classification and comparison of facial characteristics. Devices are now available which enable a trained operator, with the aid of a witness, to form a composite picture of a suspect's face and to translate that composite into a numerical code. Further developments in this area are possible, using computers to develop efficient sequences of questions so that witnesses may quickly arrive at the proper description.

Recent studies of voice analysis and synthesis, originally motivated by problems of efficient telephone transmission, have led to the development of the audio-frequency profile or "voice print." Each voice print may be sufficiently unique to permit development of a classification system that will make possible positive identification of the source of a voice print. This method of identification, using an expert to identify the voice patterns, has been introduced in more than 40 cases by 15 different police departments. As with all identification systems that rely on experts to perform the identification, controlled laboratory tests are needed to establish with care the relative frequency of errors of omission and commission made by experts.

12. The MOST appropriate title for the above passage is 12.___
    A. TECHNOLOGY IN MODERN INVESTIGATIVE DETECTION
    B. IDENTIFICATION BY PHYSICAL FEATURES
    C. VERIFICATION OF IDENTIFICATIONS BY EXPERTS
    D. THE USE OF ELECTRONIC IDENTIFICATION TECHNIQUES

13. According to the above passage, computers may be used in conjunction with which of the following identification techniques? 13.___
    A. Fingerprints
    B. Bertillon System
    C. Voice prints
    D. Composite facial pictures

14. According to the above passage, the ability to identify individuals based on facial characteristics has improved as a result of 14.___
    A. an increase in the number of facial types which can be shown to witnesses
    B. information which is derived from other body measurements
    C. coded classification and comparison techniques
    D. greater reliance upon experts to make the identifications

15. According to the above passage, it is CORRECT to state that audio-frequency profiles or *voice prints* 15.___
   A. have been decisive in many prosecutions
   B. reduce the number of errors made by experts
   C. developed as a result of problems in telephonic communications
   D. are unlikely to result in positive identifications

Questions 16-20.

DIRECTIONS: Questions 16 through 20 are to be answered SOLELY on the basis of the following graph.

EMPLOYMENT APPLICATION INFORMATION
CHECKED BY INVESTIGATORS IN DEPARTMENT Z
CENTRAL CITY

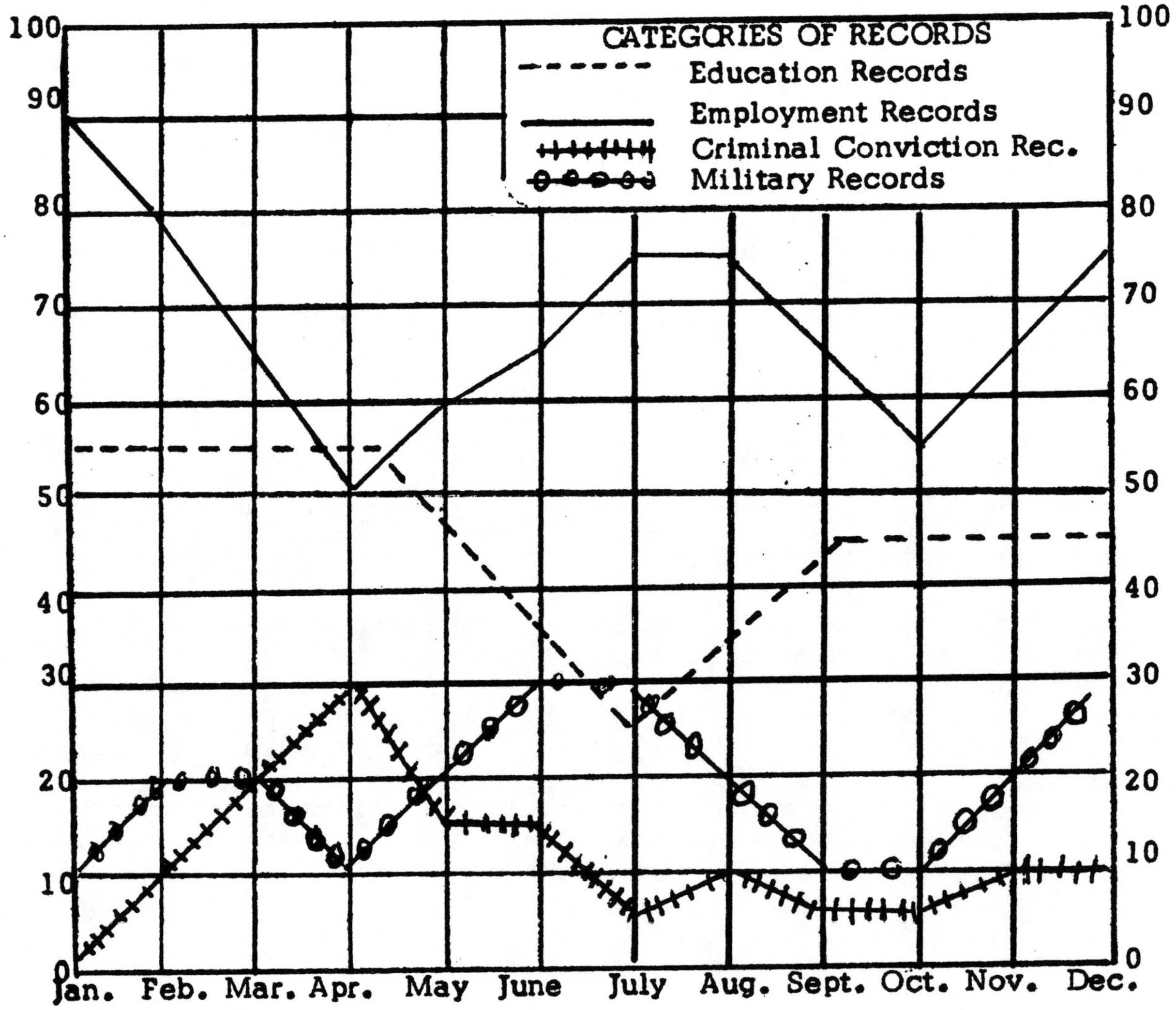

16. The category for which the SMALLEST number of record checks was made in _____ records. 16.___
A. education B. employment
C. criminal conviction D. military

17. In which of the following months did the combined number of criminal conviction record checks and military record checks EXCEED the number of education record checks? 17.___
A. March B. April C. May D. June

18. During which of the following months was the total number of records checked LARGEST? 18.___
A. March B. April
C. September D. November

19. Which of the following statements is INCORRECT according to the graph? 19.___
A. Employment records checked each month always exceeded 45.
B. Education records checked in February did not equal the number of education records checked in November.
C. Military records checked per month increased from October to December.
D. Criminal conviction records checked in any given month never exceeded the number of military records checked.

20. Of the total number of records checked in March, the percentage that were education records was MOST NEARLY 20.___
A. 13% B. 25% C. 34% D. 41%

Questions 21-25.

DIRECTIONS: Questions 21 through 25 are to be answered SOLELY on the basis of the information contained in the following tables.

STATUS OF TAX CASES ASSIGNED TO INVESTIGATORS, FISCAL YEAR, CENTRAL CITY, DEPARTMENT Y

Investigator	Cases Assigned	Cases Completed	Cases Pending at End of Fiscal Year
Albert	70	50	20
Bennett	90	60	30
Gordon	82	50	32
Nolton	70	40	30
Paxton	75	50	25
Rich	80	60	20

STATUS OF MISCELLANEOUS CASES ASSIGNED TO INVESTIGATORS
FISCAL YEAR, CENTRAL CITY, DEPARTMENT Y

Investigator	Cases Assigned	Cases Completed	Cases Pending at End of Fiscal Year
Albert	25	20	5
Bennett	20	15	5
Gordon	18	13	5
Nolton	30	23	7
Paxton	17	17	0
Rich	32	24	6

21. Of the following, the investigator who completed the GREATEST percentage of his assigned tax cases in the fiscal year was 21.____
    A. Albert B. Gordon C. Paxton D. Rich

22. The total number of the tax cases assigned in the fiscal year EXCEEDED the total number of miscellaneous cases assigned by 22.____
    A. 142 B. 325 C. 400 D. 467

23. Of the following, the two investigators who completed the SAME percentage of the miscellaneous cases assigned to them were 23.____
    A. Albert and Gordon
    B. Gordon and Nolton
    C. Nolton and Paxton
    D. Bennett and Rich

24. The average number of cases (both tax and miscellaneous) pending per investigator at the end of the fiscal year was MOST NEARLY 24.____
    A. 31 B. 28 C. 26 D. 5

25. Assume that the total number of miscellaneous cases pending at the end of the fiscal year is equal to 25% of the number of cases pending at the end of the previous fiscal year. 25.____
    What was the TOTAL number of miscellaneous cases pending at the end of the previous fiscal year?
    A. 28 B. 56 C. 74 D. 112

26. The head of an agency, in addressing a group of investigators, stated, *Whenever possible, do all you can to satisfy the needs of members of the public.* 26.____
    Which of the following is the LEAST acceptable procedure for investigators to use in implementing this policy?
    A. Handle public grievances and frustrations before they can accumulate.
    B. Satisfy public demands even though organizational goals may be compromised.
    C. Interpret rules and regulations reasonably.
    D. Use mass media to enlist support of programs to win public cooperation.

27. Of the following, the MOST important purpose of having a citizen advisory committee in a public agency is to 27.____
   A. make both the citizen groups and the public agency more responsive to the total public interest
   B. prevent fraud and mismanagement within the administration of the agency
   C. improve efficiency and encourage greater diligence on the part of agency personnel
   D. prevent the spread of unfavorable publicity about the agency's activities

28. Of the following, the term *public relations* in its application to any public agency is BEST defined as 28.____
   A. all the publicity received by the agency
   B. all the direct and indirect contacts between the agency itself and the clientele it deals with
   C. the sum total of efforts which the agency directs toward performing its functions
   D. de-emphasis of the agency's basic obligations which are not popular with its clientele

29. Assume that you receive a phone call from a man who refuses to identify himself and insists that he *knows for a fact* that an investigator on the staff of your agency has destroyed incriminating records upon receipt of a bribe. 29.____
The MOST appropriate action for you to take would be to
   A. refuse to discuss the matter unless the caller gives you his name and additional identification
   B. ask the caller for the facts and the name of the suspected investigator
   C. advise the caller that such a serious charge should be reported immediately to the police department
   D. politely advise the caller to report the facts in a letter to your agency head

30. In a public agency, the FIRST step in adopting a system which will give citizens an opportunity to make complaints against the agency's staff members is to 30.____
   A. establish an adequate complaint procedure
   B. design a citizen complaint report form
   C. establish physical facilities where complaints to the agency may be received
   D. initiate a public relations campaign informing the public that they may file complaints

31. Which of the following kinds of information is NOT found in the Official Directory of the City (Green Book)? 31.____
   A. The number of persons employed in each city agency
   B. A listing of police station houses and fire engine companies in each borough
   C. The names and addresses of all public high schools and city hospitals in each borough
   D. The names and addresses of federal, state, and city courts located within the city

32. An investigator should contact the State Department of Health to obtain information about persons who are licensed or qualified to practice as 32.____
A. x-ray technicians B. physiotherapists
C. chiropractors D. pharmacists

33. An employee complains that the city has refused to pay him some back salary for services he performed last year. This employee may bring legal action in the Small Claims Part if the amount of his claim does NOT exceed 33.____
A. $1,000 B. $1,500 C. $300 D. $100

34. Experienced investigators have found that using the question-and-answer method in interviewing a witness, instead of allowing the witness to tell his own story freely and without interruption, MOST often tends to _____ the accuracy of the information given by the witness. 34.____
A. *increase* both the scope and
B. *increase* the scope but *decrease*
C. *decrease* both the scope and
D. *decrease* the scope but *increase*

35. Of the following, the STRONGEST indication that the signature on an important document is a forgery is that the suspected signature 35.____
A. is partly illegible
B. shows a noticeable trembling in certain letters
C. shows that the writer retouched several letters
D. is identical in all respects with a signature known to be genuine

36. Prior to writing the complete and final report at the conclusion of an important case, some investigators prepare an outline or blueprint of the investigative data compiled. 36.____
All of the following are important advantages of preparing such an outline or blueprint EXCEPT that it
A. results in the omission of less important or minor facts
B. helps in achieving logical arrangement of the materials
C. lessens chances of omitting essential facts
D. aids in recognizing irrelevant details

37. In determining the validity of a document, the use of oblique lighting renders certain kinds of alterations visible. 37.____
Which of the following alterations would NOT be exposed by use of the oblique lighting technique?
A. Abrasions and erasures made in order to change some significant part of a document
B. Rubber-stamp impressions intended to validate a document but made from a non-genuine stamp
C. Tears, mutilations, or excessive foldings made deliberately in order to conceal or obscure some damaging feature of the document

D. Traced writing or writing taken from some pattern or model of genuine writing

38. When an investigator takes the witness stand for the prosecution, he must realize that the opposing counsel will GENERALLY endeavor to portray him as a(n) 38.____

A. individual whose moral character is questionable and whose veracity therefore should be doubted
B. disinterested collector and retailer of facts
C. interested party who is trying to convict his client on the basis of insufficient evidence
D. unprejudiced official with competent professional experience

39. Assume that on a certain day, an investigator finds that he has an excessive number of appointments for interviews and believes that he will be unable to keep them all during the course of the day. 39.____
Of the following, the BEST action he could take is to

A. ask a fellow investigator to help him conduct a group interview
B. interview the maximum number that can be interviewed properly and reschedule the others for a future date
C. proceed according to the established schedule
D. shorten the length of time spent interviewing each person in order to insure that everyone is interviewed

40. There has been a tendency in recent times to publicize the use of instrumentation such as lie detectors, electronic eavesdropping devices, special cameras, and other technical devices in civil and criminal investigations. 40.____
Of the following statements, the one which expresses a MAJOR weakness which results from relying too much on instrumentation as an investigative aid is:

A. The use of these technical devices invariably violates the constitutional rights of persons subject to investigations
B. Excessive publicity in the mass media about the success of these mechanical devices in solving difficult cases destroys their value as investigative aids
C. These technical devices have a very limited value in cases where abundant physical evidence is available
D. Inexperienced investigators are prone to place their faith in technical methods to the neglect of the more basic investigative procedures

KEY (CORRECT ANSWERS)

1. D	11. D	21. D	31. A
2. B	12. B	22. B	32. A
3. A	13. D	23. D	33. B
4. C	14. C	24. A	34. B
5. A	15. C	25. D	35. D
6. D	16. C	26. B	36. A
7. C	17. D	27. A	37. B
8. B	18. A	28. B	38. C
9. A	19. D	29. B	39. B
10. B	20. C	30. A	40. D

EXAMINATION SECTION

TEST 1

DIRECTIONS: Each question or incomplete statement is followed by several suggested answers or completions. Select the one that BEST answers the question or completes the statement. *PRINT THE LETTER OF THE CORRECT ANSWER IN THE SPACE AT THE RIGHT.*

1. If S, the subject that investigator H is tailing, enters a large department store, H should 1.____
   A. wait outside the store in a concealed place until S comes out
   B. follow S into the store
   C. enter the store, but wait by the door
   D. wait outside the store but in a position near the door S entered

2. Which of the following is MOST likely to indicate an attempt at falsification of a particular document? 2.____
   A. Change in style of handwriting within the document
   B. Illegible writing
   C. Erasures or alterations
   D. Folds or creases in the document

3. A subject being tailed during a foot surveillance quickly turns and confronts the shadower and states, *Say Bud, are you tailing me?* 3.____
   Of the following, the MOST appropriate action for the shadower to take is to
   A. ignore the question and keep on walking
   B. admit that he is shadowing the subject but refuse to tell him why
   C. deny the accusation but give no explanations
   D. give some excuse for his presence in the form of a cover-up

4. K, an investigator, has been given the assignment of tailing S, a suspect, who will be traveling by car at night in the city. 4.____
   Of the following, the SIMPLEST way for K to carry out this surveillance would be to
   A. mark S's car beforehand so it is identifiable at night
   B. memorize the model, color, and style of S's car
   C. memorize the license plate of S's car
   D. mechanically disable S's car so it will be unusable

5. The United States Treasury Department may prove to be a valuable source of information in specialized instances. Which of the following types of information usually would NOT be in the custody of that Federal agency? 5.____
   A. Immigration records
   B. Records of licensed manufacturers of narcotics
   C. Importers and exporters records
   D. Records of persons or firms manufacturing alcohol

6. Which of the following is a writ directing that documents or records be produced in court? 6.____
   A. Writ of habeas corpus
   B. Subpoena habeas corpus
   C. Order, pro hoc vice
   D. Subpoena duces tecum

7. *Modus Operandi* is a phrase frequently used in investigative work to refer to a 7.____
   A. specific type of investigation
   B. particular policy in tracing missing persons
   C. manner in which a criminal operates
   D. series of crimes committed by more than one person

8. P, an investigator, has been assigned to interview W, a witness, concerning a minor automobile accident. Although P has made no breach of the basic rules of contact and approach, he nevertheless recognizes that he and W have a personality clash and that a natural animosity has resulted. 8.____
   Of the following, P MOST appropriately should
   A. discuss the personality problem with W and attempt to resolve the difference
   B. stop the interview on some pretext and leave in a calm and pleasant manner, allowing an associate to continue the interview
   C. ignore the personality problem and continue as though nothing had happened
   D. change the subject matter being discussed since the facts sought may be the source of the animosity

9. Assume that an investigator desires to interview W, a reluctant witness to a bribery attempt that took place several weeks previously. Assume further that the interview can take place at a location to be designated by the interviewer. 9.____
   Of the following, the place of interview should PREFERABLY be the
   A. office of the interviewer
   B. home of W
   C. office of W
   D. scene where the event took place

10. Assume that T, an investigator, is testifying in court. He does not clearly remember the details of the incident about which he is testifying. 10.____
    Of the following, the MOST appropriate action for T to take is to
    A. admit he does not remember the details and go on to the next question
    B. look at his statement previously given to the attorney interviewing him before trial
    C. refresh his memory by referring to his notebook
    D. testify to only those items he can recall

11. Assume that as an investigator you are interviewing W, a witness. During the interview, it becomes apparent that W's statements are inaccurate and at variance with the facts previously established. 11.___
In these circumstances, it would be BEST for you to
   A. tell W that his statements are inaccurate and point out how they conflict with previously established facts
   B. reword your questions and ask additional questions about the facts being discussed
   C. warn W that he may be required to testify under oath at a later date
   D. ignore W's statements if you have other information that support the facts

12. Assume that W, a witness being interviewed by you, an investigator, shows a tendency to ramble. His answers to your questions are lengthy and not responsive. 12.___
In this situation, the BEST action for you to take is to
   A. permit W to continue because at some point he will tell you the information sought
   B. tell W that he is rambling and unresponsive and that more will be accomplished if he is brief and to the point
   C. control the interview so that complete and accurate information is obtained
   D. patiently listen to W since rambling is W's style and it cannot be changed

13. Assume that an investigator is to interview a witness. Of the following, the BEST procedure for the investigator to follow in regard to the use of his notebook is to 13.___
   A. take out his notebook at the start of the interview and immediately begin taking notes
   B. memorize the important facts related during the interview and enter them after the interview has been completed
   C. advise the witness that all his answers are being taken down to insure that he will tell the truth
   D. establish rapport with the witness and ask permission to jot down various data in his notebook

14. The first duty of the investigator who has in his possession a document which may be used in evidence is to preserve it in its original condition. 14.___
Following are three actions which might constitute rules for the handling of a document:
   I. Pick up the document with tweezers or a pin
   II. Staple the document to a folder so that it is protected
   III. Photograph or photocopy the document
Which one of the following choices MOST accurately classifies the above statements into those which are APPROPRIATE and those which are NOT APPROPRIATE as procedures for handling such documents?

A. I and III are appropriate, but II is not appropriate.
B. I and II are appropriate, but III is not appropriate.
C. II is appropriate, but I and III are not appropriate.
D. III is appropriate, but I and II are not appropriate.

15. Of the following, which one would be the CLEAREST indication that a suspicious check is a forgery? 15.___
A. There are smudges from carbon paper at the edges of the back of the check.
B. The signature on the check is an exact duplicate of an authentic signature.
C. The amount of the check has been crossed out and a new amount written in.
D. Two different color inks were used in making out the check.

16. Assume an investigator is making an inspection of a desk and finds a writing pad on which a suspect may have written. The top page of the pad has indentations which were formed when the previous page was written on. Following are three procedures which might be appropriate in order to read the indentation: 16.___
I. Hold the paper in such a manner that a single light source falls along the sheet at a parallel or oblique angle.
II. Soak the pad in water and thoroughly dry it in the sun.
III. Rub a piece of carbon paper lightly across the underside of the paper in question.
Which one of the following choices classifies the above statements into those which are APPROPRIATE procedures and those which are NOT APPROPRIATE?
A. I and II are appropriate, but III is not appropriate.
B. II and III are appropriate, but I is not appropriate.
C. I and III are appropriate, but II is not appropriate.
D. II is appropriate, but I and III are not appropriate.

17. In order to conduct an effective interview, an interviewer's attention must be continuously directed in two ways, toward himself as well as toward the interviewee. Of the following, the PRIMARY danger in this division of attention is that the 17.___
A. interviewer's behavior may become less natural and thus alienate the interviewee
B. interviewee's span of attention will be shortened
C. interviewer's response may be interpreted by the interviewee as being antagonistic
D. interviewee's more or less concealed prejudices will come to the surface

18. X and Y go into a vault together and close the door. A shot is heard, and Y rushes out with a smoking gun in his hand. 18.___
A witness to his event who said *Y shot X* would be offering
A. direct evidence B. real evidence
C. circumstantial evidence D. hearsay evidence

19. Assume that an investigator is attempting to get a suspect to agree to take a lie detector or polygraph test. 19.___
Which of the following actions on the part of the investigator would be LEAST appropriate?
   A. Describe the test to the suspect in simple language so that he understands the procedure.
   B. Suggest that the test is a means for the suspect to indicate his innocence.
   C. Discuss the test's capability of indicating whether a person is telling the truth.
   D. Suggest that a refusal to take the test indicates guilt.

20. The term *corpus delicti* is MOST appropriately used to refer to 20.___
   A. a body of criminal law
   B. the body of a person
   C. a body of civil law
   D. the body of a crime

21. Which of the following is considered the BEST type of permanent ink to use in preparing documents? 21.___
   A. Ball point
   B. Nigrosine
   C. Log wood
   D. Iron gallotannate

22. An important aspect of investigative work is the preservation of materials which may be used as evidence. 22.___
Following are three statements which might constitute rules for the proper handling of blood in a fluid condition found at a crime scene:
   I. The blood should be removed with an eye dropper and placed in a test tube.
   II. Saline solution should be added to the blood sample in a ratio of 1 to 4.
   III. The sample blood should be frozen and delivered to the laboratory as soon as possible.
Which of the following choices classifies the above actions into those which are APPROPRIATE and those which are INAPPROPRIATE?
   A. I and II are appropriate, but III is inappropriate.
   B. I and III are appropriate, but II is inappropriate.
   C. I is appropriate, but II and III are inappropriate.
   D. III is appropriate, but I and II are inappropriate.

23. The term *entrapment* refers to the act of 23.___
   A. peace officers or agents of the government in inducing a person to commit a crime not contemplated by him for the purpose of instituting a criminal prosecution against him
   B. private individuals inducing a person to commit an act not contemplated by him for the purpose of bringing a civil action against him
   C. peace officers or agents of the government in observing a person engaged in the commission of a criminal act and, therefore, obtaining direct evidence against the person
   D. private individuals or investigators in interrupting a person engaged in committing a criminal act

24. Assume you are investigating a person who is alleged to be an officer in a manufacturing corporation doing business in New York City. 24.___
Which of the following sources of information is the LEAST appropriate source to consult in checking whether this is true?
A. POOR'S REGISTER OF DIRECTORS AND EXECUTIVES
B. POLK'S BANKER'S ENCYCLOPEDIA
C. MOODY'S MANUAL OF INVESTMENTS, AMERICAN AND FOREIGN
D. POLK'S COPARTNERSHIP AND CORPORATION DIRECTORY

25. If an investigator is assigned to the surveillance of a suspect which requires the use of an automobile, it would generally be LEAST advisable for him to use a car 25.___
A. rented from a rental agency
B. personally owned by the investigator
C. bearing special unregistered plates
D. borrowed by someone who is trustworthy but has no official associations

KEY (CORRECT ANSWERS)

1. B
2. C
3. D
4. A
5. A

6. D
7. C
8. B
9. A
10. C

11. B
12. C
13. D
14. A
15. B

16. C
17. A
18. C
19. D
20. D

21. D
22. A
23. A
24. B
25. B

TEST 2

DIRECTIONS: Each question or incomplete statement is followed by several suggested answers or completions. Select the one that BEST answers the question or completes the statement. *PRINT THE LETTER OF THE CORRECT ANSWER IN THE SPACE AT THE RIGHT.*

1. Following are three statements regarding writing instruments: 1.___
   I. The hardness of the lead and the sharpness of the point affect the appearance of pencil writing.
   II. The ballpoint pen obscures the writer's ability to exhibit his characteristic habits of quality, rhythm, and shading.
   III. An examination of writing performed with a ballpoint pen easily reveals the angle at which the pen was held with relation to the writer's body and the paper.

   Which of the following choices classifies the above statements into those which are generally CORRECT and those which are generally INCORRECT?
   A. I is correct, but II and III are incorrect.
   B. II is correct, but I and III are incorrect.
   C. I and II are correct, but III is incorrect.
   D. I and III are correct, but II is incorrect.

2. Following are three statements regarding procedures to be followed in obtaining exemplars from a suspect which may or may not be appropriate: 2.___
   I. After the suspect is seated and provided with writing materials, the investigator should dictate the comparison text, always indicating punctuation and paragraphing.
   II. The material should be dictated several times, the speed of the dictation being increased each time so that the suspect will be inclined to lapse into his normal handwriting habits.
   III. As each sheet is completed, it should be removed from the suspect so that he will not be able to imitate the first exemplars he has prepared.

   Which of the following choices classifies the above procedures into those which are APPROPRIATE and those which are INAPPROPRIATE?
   A. I and II are appropriate, but III is inappropriate.
   B. I and III are appropriate, but II is inappropriate.
   C. I is appropriate, but II and III are inappropriate.
   D. III is appropriate, but I and II are inappropriate.

3. During an investigation, it may be necessary to take a *deposition*. 3.___

   The one of the following which BEST describes a *deposition* is
   A. a record made of the case progress
   B. a statement made by a witness in which he agrees to give testimony in court without resort to subpoena

C. testimony of a witness reduced to writing under oath or affirmation, in answer to interrogatories
D. another name for an *affidavit*

4. Examination of handwriting on the basis of comparing the outer shapes of letters is known as the _____ method. 4.___
A. holographic
B. penographic
C. calligraphic
D. pedographic

5. An investigator who receives a lead from an anonymous phone caller would generally be BEST advised to 5.___
A. ignore the information as unfounded
B. tell the informant to call back when he is ready to divulge his identity
C. determine from the informant the motivation behind his making the call
D. get all relevant information possible on the assumption he will not hear from the caller again

6. In order to demonstrate his findings to the court, a document examiner must use enlarged, mounted photographs. Which of the following should ALSO be submitted to the court? 6.___
A. Color enlargements, as well as black and white
B. Normal-size photographs of the enlarged documents
C. Negatives of the enlarged photographs
D. Duplicates of the enlarged photographs

7. X, an investigator, has come upon a few documents belonging to Y, a person whom X is investigating. The documents cannot be taken or moved. 7.___
Of the following, the MOST appropriate action for X to take is to
A. make a record of the documents, making certain to include any names, addresses, and numbers mentioned even though they may appear meaningless at the time of discovery
B. make a record only of those documents deemed relevant by him at the time of discovery, including names, addresses, and numbers mentioned
C. leave the documents without making any notes because documents that cannot be moved may not be copied
D. make a record only of those names, addresses, or numbers mentioned which are clearly relevant to the case

8. Assume that you are interviewing W, a neighbor of N, whom you are investigating. It is important to establish whether or not N uses alcoholic beverages excessively. 8.___
Which of the following questions is MOST appropriate for obtaining the information you seek?
A. Have you ever seen N intoxicated?
B. Can you tell me something about N's habits?
C. Do you know whether or not N is a patron of nearby bars?
D. What is N's reputation in the neighborhood?

9. A check may be altered to change the amount, the name, or some other element. 9.___
The one of the following which can BEST be used to discover any changes is
A. a magnetometer
B. an ultra-violet lamp
C. a tensimeter
D. polarography

10. Z, an investigator, is attempting to interview W concerning an accident witnessed by W. However, W is disinterested and indifferent. 10.___
In order to encourage W's cooperation, Z should
A. stimulate W's interest by stressing the importance of the information that he possesses
B. impress upon W that Z is an investigator performing an official function
C. warn W that the withholding of information may be considered as an obstruction of justice
D. gain W's sympathy for Z, who is merely trying to do his job

11. Of the following, the three types of ink MOST commonly used in the United States today are: 11.___
A. gallotannic, logwood, and nigrosine
B. gallotannic, vanadium, and wolfram
C. wolfram, logwood, and nigrosine
D. vanadium, logwood, and nigrosine

12. Which of the following BEST describes the science of poroscopy? 12.___
Identification
A. by the casting of footprints
B. by the tracing of tools used in a crime
C. by means of sweat pores indicated on a fingerprint
D. through the examination of human hairs

13. Which of the following statements concerning the folding of paper is generally ACCURATE? 13.___
A. When uncut paper has been folded, the fibers remain unbroken.
B. If an ink line is first drawn and the paper is subsequently folded, the line over the fold will not be even and uniform.
C. If an ink line is written over an already existing fold, the ink will spread over the fold but protruding fibers will not become stained.
D. It is almost impossible to determine whether a lead pencil line was drawn on a paper before or after it was folded.

14. All of the following are generally good methods of making erased lead-pencil writing visible EXCEPT 14.___
A. examination in non-polarized light
B. use of iodine fumes
C. contrast photography
D. photography in oblique light

15. Following are four statements concerning crime-scene photography that may or may not be valid: 15.___
   I. The general procedure of crime-scene photography aims at obtaining views of broad areas of the crime locale, supplemented by closer views of sections containing important detail.
   II. The crime scene should be first photographed in its original, undisturbed state.
   III. Crime-scene photographs are of great value to the investigator because they accurately show the distances between objects.
   IV. If a room is to be photographed, a set of at least four views will be required to show the room adequately.

   Which of the following choices MOST accurately classifies the above into those which are VALID procedures and those which are NOT VALID?
   A. I and II are valid, but III and IV are not valid.
   B. I, II, and IV are valid, but III is not valid.
   C. III and IV are valid, but I and II are not valid.
   D. I, II, and III are valid, but IV is not valid.

16. Following are four statements concerning the erasing of ink which may or may not be valid: 16.___
   I. It may be difficult to detect an erasure made with an eradicator, especially after a considerable length of time has elapsed.
   II. When an erasure has been made with a knife or rubber, it is generally easy to detect the area involved, as it is translucent.
   III. The sulfocyanic acid method is inappropriate for the detection of residue of iron-containing inks.
   IV. Examination with ultra-violet rays should not be strongly relied upon because clever forgers have been known to wash away all residue of eradication with distilled water.

   Which of the following choices MOST accurately classifies the above statements into those which are generally VALID and those which are NOT VALID?
   A. I and II are generally valid, but III and IV are not generally valid.
   B. IV is generally valid, but I, II, and III are not generally valid.
   C. I, II, and IV are generally valid, but III is not generally valid.
   D. III and IV are generally valid, but I and II are not generally valid.

17. Following are four statements concerning fingerprints which may or may not be true: 17.___
   I. Plastic fingerprints are found on such objects as a bar of soap or ball of melted wax.
   II. Visible fingerprints are left by fingers covered with a colored material such as blood or grease.

III. The majority of latent fingerprints are relatively invisible and must be developed.
IV. Dirty surfaces and absorbent materials readily bear prints.

Which of the following choices MOST accurately classifies the above statements into those which are TRUE and those which are NOT TRUE?

A. I and II are true; III and IV are not true.
B. I and III are true; II and IV are not true.
C. I, II, and III are true, and IV is not true.
D. I, II, and IV are true, and III is not true.

18. Of the following, the method of fingerprint classification MOST commonly used in the United States is the _____ system. 18.___

A. Henry B. Vucetich C. Bertillon D. Pottecher

19. Of the following, the term *curtilage* is MOST appropriately used to refer to 19.___

A. the enclosed space of ground and buildings immediately surrounding a dwelling
B. a surgical procedure used to induce an abortion
C. the illegal detention of suspects by law enforcement personnel
D. a legal action taken by a judge to curtail the irrelevant testimony of witnesses in court

20. Which of the following statements is MOST valid as a guide to investigators in their dealings with informants? 20.___

A. Whether they are agreeable or not, informants should be made available for questioning by other agencies since they may have good information in areas other than those which directly concern you.
B. Many informants work out of revenge, while some others do it only for money. Therefore, you should evaluate the information they give you with regard to their motivation.
C. Informants tend to use their connections with law enforcement agencies. From time to time, they must be put in their place by letting them know they are *stool pigeons*.
D. To cultivate informants, it is a good practice to give them some money in advance so they will be assured of a reward when they have good information.

21. The more meager the evidence against a suspect, the later the suspect should be allowed to know of it. 21.___
As a practical rule to guide the investigator during an interrogation, the advice contained in this statement is GENERALLY

A. *bad*, chiefly because suspects have a right to know the details of the offense being investigated
B. *good*, chiefly because the interrogator will not look foolish due to his lack of information

C. *bad*, chiefly because the investigator will be unable to develop the proper rapport with the suspect during the interrogation
D. *good*, chiefly because the suspect, not sensing the direction of the interrogation, is more likely to reveal information

22. Following are three statements concerning fingerprinting which may or may not be valid: 22.___
I. The best paper for fingerprinting purposes has a rough surface which will absorb ink.
II. The subject should roll his fingers on the paper from right to left exercising as much pressure as possible on the paper to make a print.
III. Fingerprints taken with stamp-pad ink are not usually legible or permanent.
Which of the following classifies the above statements into thos which are VALID and those which are NOT VALID?
A. I is valid, but II and III are not valid.
B. I and II are valid, but III is not valid.
C. II is valid, but I and III are not valid.
D. III is valid, but I and II are not valid.

23. All of the following statements concerning fingerprints are true EXCEPT: 23.___
A. There are no two identical fingerprints
B. Fingerprint patterns are not generally changed by illness
C. A modern procedure called dactylmogrification has been developed to change the fingerprints of individuals relatively easily
D. if the skin on the fingertips is wounded, the whole fingerprint pattern will reappear when the wound heals

24. Mechanical erasures on a document produce an abrasion of the paper. Assume that a forger makes an ink writing which crosses an area which has been previously erased. Following are three conditions which might result in the erased area from such an action: 24.___
I. The ink line is brighter.
II. The ink line is wider.
III. The ink line tends to run or feather out sideways.
Which one of the following choices MOST accurately classifies the above statements into those which would result from writing over the erased area and those which would not?
A. I and II would result, but III would not result.
B. I and III would result, but II would not result.
C. II would result, but I and III would not result.
D. II and III would result, but I would not result.

25. In the investigation of the periodic theft of equipment from stockrooms, the detection of the thieves is USUALLY accomplished by 25.___
   A. the use of strict inventory controls
   B. careful background investigation of applicants for the stockroom jobs
   C. issuing photo identification cards to all employees of the agency
   D. the use of intelligent surveillance

KEY (CORRECT ANSWERS)

1. C
2. D
3. C
4. C
5. D

6. B
7. A
8. A
9. B
10. A

11. A
12. C
13. D
14. A
15. B

16. C
17. C
18. A
19. A
20. B

21. D
22. D
23. C
24. D
25. D

EXAMINATION SECTION
TEST 1

DIRECTIONS: Each question or incomplete statement is followed by several suggested answers or completions. Select the one that BEST answers the question or completes the statement. *PRINT THE LETTER OF THE CORRECT ANSWER IN THE SPACE AT THE RIGHT.*

1. Which of the following statements concerning the questioning of a witness by an investigator is VALID? 1.___
   A. The investigator should insist on *yes* and *no* answers from a witness because such responses insure accurate answers.
   B. The investigator should ask questions which suggest answers in order to speed the flow of information from the witness.
   C. Long and complicated questions should be used to impress the witness with the perceptiveness and intelligence of the investigator, thus insuring the cooperation of the witness.
   D. The investigator may be able to distinguish between honest mistakes and intended misrepresentations made by a witness by rewording his queries and by asking additional questions.

2. Following are three statements concerning interviewing and investigative practice: 2.___
   I. In order to improve his ability to interview persons successfully, the investigator should evaluate his performance during and after each interview
   II. An investigator who has detected evasiveness in the statements of a subject should write off these remarks as of little value to his investigation, and need not attempt to substantiate them
   III. In order to gain a psychological advantage over a difficult witness in an interview, it would be good practice for an investigator to ask the subject to sit in a chair other than the one the subject has selected

   Which of the following CORRECTLY classifies the above statements into those which are correct and those which are not?
   A. III is correct, but I and II are not.
   B. I is correct, but II and III are not.
   C. I and III are correct, but II is not.
   D. II and III are correct, but I is not.

3. An investigator, following a subject under surveillance, boards the same bus that the subject has just entered. If the subject suddenly jumps off before it starts, the investigator should 3.____
   A. stay on the bus, get off at the next stop, and wait for the next bus
   B. attempt to get off the bus before it starts
   C. stay on the bus, get off the next stop, and take another bus or taxi back to the original stop
   D. assume that he has been spotted and discontinue any further attempts to follow the subject

4. The technique of taking a written statement of the information the investigator obtains from a witness and then having the witness sign the statement is 4.____
   A. *useful*, because a written statement presented to the court is more acceptable than oral testimony from that witness
   B. *not useful*, because the witness will be intimidated
   C. *useful*, because the witness may forget or change his version of what happened at a later time
   D. *not useful*, because it delays the investigator's handling of the case

5. For evidence to be admissible in court, it must be 5.____
   A. relevant but not necessarily material
   B. material and relevant
   C. of sufficient weight to influence any judicial decision or determination
   D. of sufficient weight to be material

6. Which of the following statements BEST describes the term *judicial notice*? 6.____
   The
   A. act by which a court recognizes the truth of certain facts without the formal presentation of evidence
   B. method by which a court notifies an individual that he is indicted
   C. process by which notice of court action is given to the general public
   D. communication of notice of court action, orally or in writing, directly to the affected person or the party to be charged

7. Assume that you are a supervising investigator interviewing a witness to alleged employee corruption. In replying to a question on bribe-taking, the subject shifts to a totally unrelated topic. 7.____
   Of the following, the BEST way to determine why the witness seems to be evading the question is to pursue the questioning
   A. *aggressively*, chiefly because the subject is probably an unwilling accomplice to misconduct
   B. *aggressively*, chiefly because the subject is probably protecting a fellow employee

C. *tactfully*, chiefly because the subject is probably unaware of any wrongdoing
D. *tactfully*, chiefly because the subject is probably withholding information that embarrasses him

8. An investigator usually develops positive or negative rapport with individuals he interviews. 8.____
When this occurs, the investigator should
A. control the nature and intensity of the relationship
B. direct his total attention to finishing the interview
C. develop a passive, professional attitude toward the interviewee
D. appear personally friendly to eliminate any negative feelings the interviewee may have

9. Which of the following techniques is MOST effective in detecting erasures on a document? 9.____
A. Look for an abrupt change in the style of writing
B. Examine the spacing of letters to see whether there has been crowding
C. Hold the document approximately edgewise to a light, close to the edge of the light's shade, and look for damaged paper fibers
D. Fume the document with the chemical vapors of gallotannate or nigrosine acid, which react with ink's residue

10. At times, an investigator may ask a subject for samples of his handwriting for purposes of comparison with a questioned document. 10.____
When taking such samples, which of the following procedures should be AVOIDED?
A. Placing the subject in a quiet place under minimal acceptable observation
B. Having the subject write something other than a list of signatures
C. Having the subject copy written or printed material
D. Removing each sample before the next one is started

11. Which of the following can PROPERLY be classified as *secondary* evidence? 11.____
A. Altered time sheets of accused employees
B. Eyewitness testimony regarding time and leave abuses
C. Official payroll roster records
D. Photocopies of forged checks

12. Following are three statements describing possible characteristics of fraudulent checks: 12.____
I. The first endorsement is clearly signed, matches the payee's name on the front, and appears right above the second endorsement
II. The name of the bank on which the check is drawn and its location are abbreviated on the face of the check
III. The digit and written amount of the check correspond exactly, and the payer's account number is inked over

Which of the following CORRECTLY classifies the above statements into those that describe characteristics generally peculiar to fraudulent checks and those that do not?

A. I and II are characteristic, but III is not.
B. I is a characteristic, but II and III are not.
C. II and III are characteristic, but I is not.
D. III is a characteristic, but I and II are not.

13. Following are four statements concerning communication between an investigator and an informant: 13.___

I. Meetings between an investigator and an informant should be held at the investigator's office
II. The proper name of the informant should not be used when telephoning
III. The investigator's organization should not be identified in any correspondence with the informant
IV. The circumstances surrounding meetings between the investigator and an informant should be repeated to establish a pattern

Which one of the following choices CORRECTLY classifies the above statements into those which are valid and those which are not valid as procedures for handling communications with an informant?

A. I and II are valid, but III and IV are not valid.
B. II and III are valid, but I and IV are not valid.
C. III is valid, but I, II, and IV are not valid.
D. IV is valid, but I, II, and III are not valid.

14. Of the following, the IMMEDIATE objective of an investigator, while speaking on the telephone to an anonymous person who is voluntarily offering information, should be to 14.___

A. form an estimate of the informant's reliability
B. decide on the motives and interests of the informer
C. draw out all relevant information before the informer hangs up
D. compare this information with that obtained from other sources

15. Supervising investigators are often called upon to provide subordinate investigators with on-the-job training. Following are three statements concerning the administration of on-the-job training: 15.___

I. The supervisor selected to provide training must be an outstanding performer of the job he is teaching.
II. The supervisor should have access to information about the training needs of the investigators he is to train.
III. The subordinate investigators should be assigned to the work stations in which they will ultimately be employed.

Which of the following CORRECTLY classifies the above statements into those that are appropriate practices and those that are not?

A. I is appropriate, but II and III are not.
B. III is appropriate, but I and II are not.
C. I and III are appropriate, but II is not.
D. II and III are appropriate, but I is not.

16. Assume you are training a group of new investigators and that one member of the group is a slower learner than the others. 16.____
Of the following, the BEST way to handle this situation is to
A. adapt your instruction speed to the rate of the slowest learner in order to reduce the possibility of frustrating him
B. instruct at the level that is best suited to the majority of the group and give the slow learner individual help after the regular training sessions
C. teach at the level at which you are most comfortable and handle problems as you become aware of them
D. adjust your instruction speed to that of the slowest learner and provide him with extra remedial exercises or practice work

17. The one of the following that is a DISADVANTAGE of the conference approach to training investigators is that 17.____
A. each investigator's ideas are critically evaluated by the other group members
B. the informal atmosphere prevents the development of close relationships among investigators
C. group members have time to reflect only on their own contributions and not on those of other investigators
D. many investigators lack the skills or discipline to benefit from such training

18. Standard methods for performing various investigative tasks are useful MAINLY because they 18.____
A. permit the supervisor to reduce the total time he spends on planning
B. eliminate the need for monitoring costs
C. enable the supervisor to spend less time on routine and detail
D. reduce the number of forms needed to complete the tasks

19. Assume that, in one agency, the average number of absences per employee varies greatly from one investigative unit to another but the physical working conditions and type of work performed are similar in each of these units. 19.____
Of the following, the MOST probable cause of the differences in the amount of absenteeism is the
A. educational background of the employees
B. number of female employees in the agency
C. attitudes of the supervisors
D. existence of an agency medical unit

20. In order to learn their job properly, newly hired investigators must receive an indication from their supervisors of the quality of their performance. The one of the following techniques that provides the MOST constructive *feedback* from supervisors to their subordinates is 20.___
A. praising all aspects of subordinates' performance
B. pointing out to subordinates that mistakes may result in poor probationary reports
C. drawing the subordinates' attention to how close their performance is to the expected level of performance
D. preparing written critiques for study by subordinates

21. Of the following, the BEST way for a supervisor to reduce absenteeism within his unit is to 21.___
A. inform subordinates that all excuses due to illness will be referred to the personnel officer
B. discuss with individual employees the reasons for their absences
C. assign less desirable work to those absent most often
D. recommend that employees who are absent most often be transferred to other units

22. Of the following, the MOST important factor in determining whether a supervisor is a success or a failure as a manager is his ability to 22.___
A. do all work assigned to his unit better than his subordinates can
B. make suggestions which are acceptable to top management
C. train employees for various responsibilities
D. delegate work so that it is performed effectively

Questions 23-25.

DIRECTIONS: Below is a report consisting of 15 numbered sentences, some of which are not consistent with the principles of good report writing. Answer Questions 23 through 25 SOLELY on the basis of the information contained in the report and your knowledge of investigative principles and practices.

To: Tom Smith, Administrative Investigator
From: John Jones, Supervising Investigator

1. On January 7, I received a call from Mrs. H. Harris of 684 Sunset Street, Brooklyn.
2. Mrs. Harris informed me that she wanted to report an instance of fraud relating to public assistance payments being received by her neighbor, Mrs. I Wallace.
3. I advised her that such a subject would best be discussed in person.
4. I then arranged a field visitation for January 10 at Mrs. Harris' apartment, 684 Sunset Street, Brooklyn.

5. On January 10, I discussed the basis for Mrs. Harris' charge against Mrs. Wallace at the former's apartment.
6. She stated that her neighbor is receiving Aid to Dependent Children payments for seven children, but that only three of her children are still living with her.
7. In addition, Mrs. Harris also claimed that her husband, whom she reported to the authorities as missing, usually sees her several times a week.
8. After further questioning, Mrs. Harris admitted to me that she had been quite friendly with Mrs. Wallace until they recently argued about trash left in their adjoining hall corridor.
9. However, she firmly stated that her allegations against Mrs. Wallace were valid and that she feared repercussions for her actions.
10. At the completion of the interview, I assured Mrs. Harris of the confidentiality of her statements and that an attempt would be made to verify her allegations.
11. As I was leaving Mrs. Harris' apartment, I noticed a man, aged approximately 45, walking out of Mrs. Wallace's apartment.
12. I followed him until he entered a late model green Oldsmobile and sped away.
13. On January 3, I returned to 684 Sunset Court, having determined that Mrs. Wallace is receiving assistance as indicated by Mrs. Harris.
14. However, upon presentation of official identification Mrs. Wallace refused to admit me to her apartment or grant an interview.
15. I am therefore referring this matter to you for further instructions.

John Jones
Supervising Investigator

23. The one of the following statements that clearly lacks vital information is statement 23.____
A. 8 B. 10 C. 12 D. 14

24. Which of the following sentences from the report is ambiguous? 24.____
Sentence
A. 2 B. 3 C. 7 D. 10

25. Which of the following sentences contains information contradicting other data in the above report? 25.____
Sentence
A. 3 B. 8 C. 10 D. 13

KEY (CORRECT ANSWERS)

1. D	6. A	11. D	16. B	21. B
2. C	7. D	12. C	17. D	22. D
3. A	8. A	13. B	18. C	23. C
4. C	9. C	14. C	19. C	24. C
5. B	10. C	15. D	20. C	25. D

EXAMINATION SECTION
TEST 1

DIRECTIONS: Each question or incomplete statement is followed by several suggested answers or completions. Select the one that BEST answers the question or completes the statement. *PRINT THE LETTER OF THE CORRECT ANSWER IN THE SPACE AT THE RIGHT.*

1. During an interview with a witness, the investigator should carefully observe the witness's gestures and facial expressions. 1.____
To interpret the meaning of these actions, the investigator should do all of the following EXCEPT to
   A. try to *read* the situation in which a puzzling gesture is used
   B. ask questions that relate specifically to the gesture
   C. take an educated guess based on past experience
   D. rely on the standard meaning of the gesture

2. Of the following, the MOST important skill for a supervisor of investigators to possess is the ability to 2.____
   A. communicate effectively
   B. obtain the respect of his staff
   C. remain calm in pressure situations
   D. develop high morale among his subordinates

3. Following are three statements concerning the preparation by an investigator of a written statement taken from a witness: 3.____
   I. Have each page initialed by the witness
   II. Correct and initial any mistakes in grammar that are made by the witness
   III. Leave space between paragraphs to facilitate the addition of notes and comments.
Which of the following correctly classifies the above statements into those that are valid and those that are not?
   A. I is valid, but II and III are not.
   B. II and III are valid, but I is not.
   C. III is valid, but I and II are not.
   D. I and II are valid, but III is not.

4. Assume, as an investigator, you are questioning an employee of your agency suspected of misstating previous work experience on his employment application. You notice that the employee is reluctant to admit that his previous statements were inaccurate. 4.____
The one of the following that is the BEST method of obtaining the truth from this employee would be for you to
   A. tell him that his job is not in jeopardy
   B. make him feel he is not being criticized

C. have him discuss the matter with your supervisor
D. allow him to correct any inaccuracies on his employment application

5. If several witnesses describing the same occurrence agree on most details, the investigator should then 5.____
A. determine whether or not these witnesses were in communication with each other
B. assume that such agreement means that the recollection was correct
C. assume that the witnesses' observations were incorrect since two or more people usually will not agree on the same details
D. question the witnesses again, concentrating on the details on which they differ

6. In trying to obtain a statement from a hospitalized individual who is unable to receive visitors, it would be BEST for an investigator to 6.____
A. draw up a statement from his own knowledge of the case and ask a hospital staff member to have the patient sign the statement when he is well
B. contact the patient's family and arrange for an appointment to see the patient as soon as his condition permits
C. leave a message at the hospital for the patient to contact him when he is available to receive visitors
D. appear at the hospital with proper identification and request official permission from the hospital administrator to speak with the patient

7. Among employment specialists, it is generally agreed that the value of character references on employment applications is 7.____
A. *limited*, chiefly because such references are written only by personal friends of the applicant
B. *significant*, chiefly because information they transmit is unavailable from other sources
C. *limited*, chiefly because they tend to give only favorable information
D. *significant*, chiefly because they have direct knowledge of the applicant's abilities

8. The MOST important requirement of a person who is testifying about a criminal act that he witnessed is that he 8.____
A. was conscious and attentive during the crime
B. is a respected and trustworthy member of the community
C. is without a prior criminal record
D. gives a consistent account of the details of the crime

9. Assume that, after taking a written statement from Employee A, an investigator is about to obtain his signature. He wants to ask Employee B, a co-worker, to witness the signing but Employee B is not available at that time. 9.____
To expedite the investigation, it would be MOST desirable for the investigator to
   A. have Employee A sign the statement and obtain Employee B's signature at a later time
   B. ask an available disinterested party to witness Employee A's signature
   C. witness Employee A's signature himself
   D. have Employee A sign when Employee B is available

10. Witnesses are usually MOST willing to discuss an event when they are 10.____
   A. disinterested in the subsequent investigation
   B. interviewed immediately following the event
   C. interviewed for the first time
   D. known by the investigator

11. To determine the former addresses of a person who has moved several times within the same locality, it would be BEST to contact 11.____
   A. the Post Office
   B. insurance companies
   C. public utilities
   D. banking institutions

12. The one of the following that is CHARACTERISTIC of the interview as compared with the observation approach to investigation is that an interview generally 12.____
   A. requires more time to complete adequately
   B. is more likely to result in incomplete information
   C. is less applicable to the study of an individual's beliefs and values
   D. is less costly to conduct

13. The use of slang on the part of an investigator when questioning subjects is generally 13.____
   A. *inadvisable*, chiefly because it leads to misinterpretations
   B. *advisable*, chiefly because it will insure objective responses
   C. *inadvisable*, chiefly because it can compromise the investigator's dignity
   D. *advisable*, chiefly because it can promote ease of speech and understanding

14. Assume that a job applicant claims on his employment application that he has just recently become a United States citizen. 14.____
Of the following, it would be MOST appropriate for you, in verifying this matter, to consult the
   A. Department of State
   B. Treasury Department
   C. Immigration and Naturalization Service
   D. Department of Justice

15. If an investigator receives an anonymous phone call from a person claiming to have knowledge of criminal behavior in an agency which is currently being investigated, the investigator should 15.___
   A. listen politely and make notes on the important facts given by the informant
   B. tell the informant what has already been discovered and ask if he has anything to add
   C. question the informant to obtain all the information he has
   D. ask the informant to submit his information in writing

16. When interviewing a child, an investigator should keep in mind the fact that children 16.___
   A. are psychologically incapable of giving an accurate statement
   B. usually have faulty perception
   C. are easily led into making incorrect statements since they tend to agree with the questioner
   D. will often make statements which are pure fantasy because they are not as observant as adults

17. Following are three statements concerning the use of an investigator's notebook in court: 17.___
   I. A looseleaf-type notebook creates a more favorable impression in the courtroom than a bound notebook because the former permits the removal of pages unrelated to the case in question
   II. An investigator's notebook should be written in ink, not pencil, because of the need for permanence
   III. The notebook should ideally contain the notes of only one investigation so that its scrutiny will not involve the disclosure of information relating to other investigations

   Which of the following CORRECTLY classifies the above statements into those which are valid and those which are not valid?
   A. I and III are valid, but II is not.
   B. I and II are valid, but III is not.
   C. I is valid, but II and III are not.
   D. II and III are valid, but I is not.

18. The first three digits of a social security number are coded for the 18.___
   A. age of the cardholder when the card was issued
   B. cardholder's initials
   C. year the card was issued
   D. area in which the card was issued

19. Two methods of obtaining personal background information are the personal interview and the telephone inquiry. As compared with the latter, the personal type of interview USUALLY _____ flexibility in questioning _____ frankness. 19.___
   A. permits; but discourages
   B. restricts; but encourages
   C. permits; and encourages
   D. restricts; and discourages

20. One of the important functions of investigators is to perform surveillances without the knowledge of the subject. If a subject thinks he is being followed, he is LEAST likely to react by 20.___
   A. reversing his course to see whether anyone else does likewise
   B. boarding a subway car and getting off just before it pulls out
   C. attempting to pass the surveillant several times to view him face-to-face
   D. using the services of a *convoy* to observe whether he is being followed

21. Assume that you are conducting an interview with a prospective employee who is of limited mental ability and low socio-economic status. Of the following, it is MOST likely that asking him many open-ended questions about his work experience would cause him to respond 21.___
   A. articulately
   B. reluctantly
   C. comfortably
   D. aggressively

22. Assume, as an investigator, you want a witness to sign a statement. Which of the following phrases is MOST likely to secure his signature? 22.___
   A. I would appreciate it if you would sign the statement at this time.
   B. Sign the statement where indicated.
   C. Sign the statement when you get the chance.
   D. If the statement is generally correct, please sign it.

23. During an interview, a subject makes statements an investigator knows to be false. Of the following, it would be MOST appropriate for the investigator to 23.___
   A. point out each inconsistency in the subject's story as soon as the investigator detects it
   B. interrupt the subject and request that he submit to a polygraph test
   C. allow the subject to continue talking until he becomes enmeshed in his lies and then confront him with his falsehoods

D. allow the subject to finish what he has to say and then explicitly inform him that it is a crime to lie to a government employee

24. One of the major objectives of a pre-employment interview is to get the interviewee to respond freely to inquiries. The one of the following actions that would be MOST likely to restrict the conversation of the interviewee would be for the investigator to 24.___
A. keep a stenographic record of the interviewee's statements
B. ask questions requiring complete explanations
C. pose direct, specific questions to the interviewee
D. allow the interviewee to respond to questions at his own pace

25. A list of the names, addresses, and titles of city employees is made available to the public by the 25.___
A. civil service commission
B. comptroller's office
C. mayor's office
D. municipal reference and research center

KEY (CORRECT ANSWERS)

1. D
2. A
3. A
4. B
5. A
6. B
7. C
8. A
9. B
10. B
11. C
12. D
13. D
14. C
15. C
16. C
17. D
18. D
19. C
20. C
21. B
22. B
23. C
24. A
25. D

MEMORY FOR FACTS AND INFORMATION

EXAMINATION SECTION

TEST 1

DIRECTIONS: Questions 1 through 15 test your ability to remember key facts and details. You are given a rather long reading passage, which you will have approximately ten minutes to read. The reading selection should then be turned over. Then immediately answer the fifteen questions that refer to this passage. Please do NOT refer back to the reading passage at any time while you are answering the questions. Select the letter that represents the BEST of the four possible choices.

THE CASE OF THE MISSING OVERTIME WAGES

Melba Tolliber is a new Labor Standards Investigator assigned to investigate a complaint of nonpayment of some overtime wages. The complaint came in the form of a telephone call from Albert Brater, employed by the Whizzer Audio and Video Store in Dorchester. Whizzer Audio and Video, Inc. is a fast-growing and very successful chain in the Northeast. Their headquarters is in Dorchester.

Melba Tolliber drives the eight miles to Dorchester on a breezy Monday morning. She meets with Albert Brater, the employee who called. He is employed in the warehouse unit.

Hello, Mr. Brater, my name is Melba Tolliber, and I'm here to investigate whether you've been paid the proper amount of overtime wages.

Nice to meet you, Ms. Tolliber. I'm not the only one with this problem. Two salesclerks in the Dorchester store, Mary and Martin, have also gotten less for overtime than they should have.

Can I talk with them, too? Melba asks.

Well, the problem is, we're worried about getting into a lot of trouble with the company. We were hoping you could talk just to me. I'm a little worried about talking with you myself.

This is a confidential interview; don't worry. It would be very helpful, however, if I could at least get copies of their paystubs.

Albert hesitates and then says, *Gee, I hope I can find my last paystub. Anyway, we've been working forty-six hours a week the last four weeks, but only getting paid our usual rate of $3.25 an hour.*

Melba says, *But that's below the minimum wage.*

Maybe it's $3.35; I get confused; I'll have to check. I think it's $3.35. Yeah, I'm pretty sure it's $3.35. But you know what else? I was promised a raise of $.50 per hour after eight months of working here, and that's up next week. We'll see if I get it or not.

Have the other employees here gotten the raises they were promised?

Yeah, I think they have. But I know of at least one person, a truckdriver, who hasn't gotten his raise yet.

Do you know his name?

Just his first name. But the next time I see him, I'll ask him if he's gotten the raise yet. I'll let you know if he hasn't.

What day would be good for you to drop off the paystubs and have a second interview?

Well, you have to give me some time to get them from Mary and Martin, too. How about this Thursday afternoon at one?

Fine, here's my card. I'll see you this Thursday at one.

At the beginning of their next meeting, Albert gives Melba the paystubs for the last month's work for all three employees.

Let's do you first, Albert. What have your hours been each week for the last four weeks?

I've worked the same schedule for the past month, my usual forty hours - 8 to 5 with an hour for lunch, which I don't like, on Mondays, Tuesdays, and Thursdays. Wednesdays and Fridays I've worked from 8 A.M. to 9 P.M. because those are the days we do our most shipping. They give us from 5 to 6 P.M. as a dinner break on those days.

So that adds up to forty-six hours. Give me a few minutes to go over these figures with my calculator.

That's a great calculator; it's so small. Looks like a credit card.

Thanks, but I have to be careful how I hit the numbers; there's not much room.... Well, according to my calculations, you're owed $40.20 in overtime pay for the last four weeks. But there's something else wrong, too. It looks like they've been taking out a little too much money for Social Security. Let me recheck this.

1. In the passage, Melba Tolliber visited 1.___
   A. Midwood
   B. Dorchester
   C. Midale
   D. Midville

2. In the passage, Melba talked with 2.___
   A. Albert who works in the warehouse unit
   B. Albert who works in the warehouse unit and in the store
   C. Robert who works in the warehouse
   D. Robert, Martin, and Mary who work in the warehouse and the store

3. The organization whose payment of overtime wages is in question 3.___
   A. is struggling to succeed
   B. is the most successful of the new audio-visual store chains in the Northeast
   C. has its headquarters in the town that Melba travels to
   D. has successfully switched from selling just records to selling records, tapes, and video equipment

4. During their initial discussion, how sure of his rate of pay was the employee to whom Melba spoke? 4.___
   A. Not sure at all
   B. Very sure
   C. Pretty sure
   D. Totally unsure

5. What day of the week did Melba conduct the initial interview? 5.___
   A. Monday
   B. Wednesday
   C. Tuesday
   D. Thursday

6. When did Melba conduct the second interview? 6.___
   A. Monday at 1 P.M.
   B. Thursday at 1 P.M.
   C. Wednesday at 1 P.M.
   D. Friday at 1 P.M.

7. In order to calculate how much money the employee should have received, Melba used a 7.___
   A. credit card
   B. calculator
   C. credit card/calculator/watch combination
   D. desk top personal computer

8. According to the passage, what did Melba do to try to make the employee feel more at ease? She 8.___
   A. gave him time to collect his thoughts
   B. assured him that she believed what he said
   C. assured him that the interview was confidential
   D. asked if she could speak with the other two employees affected

9. The initial complaint from the employee 9.___
   A. resulted in his receiving back pay
   B. came in the form of a phone call
   C. was anonymous
   D. resulted in a large-scale investigation

10. The name of the establishment the employee works for is the 10.___
   A. Whizzer
   B. Genuine Article
   C. Electronic Era
   D. Gizmos etcetera

11. The other two employees who have questions about their overtime pay 11.___
   A. are truckdrivers
   B. work in the warehouse
   C. are salesclerks
   D. work in maintenance

12. The organization told the employee he would receive a 12.___
   A. $.60 per hour raise after eight months
   B. $.60 per hour raise after five months
   C. $.50 per hour raise after six months
   D. $.50 per hour raise after eight months

13. How many hours a week have the employees who are questioning their pay been working for the last month? 13.___
   A. Forty-four
   B. Forty-five
   C. Forty-six
   D. Forty-eight

14. In the last month, what hours did the employee Melba interviewed work on Wednesdays? 14.___
   A. 8 A.M. to 5 P.M.
   B. 9 A.M. to 10 P.M.
   C. 9 A.M. to 5 P.M.
   D. 8 A.M. to 9 P.M.

15. At the start of the second interview, 15.___
   A. the employee gives Melba the paystubs for the last month for all three workers involved
   B. the employee gives Melba the paystubs for the last month for all three workers involved, with the exception of his last paystub
   C. the employee gives Melba only his paystubs from the last month
   D. it cannot be determined if the employee gives Melba any paystubs

KEY (CORRECT ANSWERS)

1. B	6. B	11. C
2. A	7. B	12. D
3. C	8. C	13. C
4. C	9. B	14. D
5. A	10. A	15. A

TEST 2

DIRECTIONS: Questions 1 through 15 test your ability to remember key facts and details. You are given a rather long reading passage, which you will have approximately ten minutes to read. The reading selection should then be turned over. Then immediately answer the fifteen questions that refer to this passage. Please do NOT refer back to the reading passage at any time while you are answering these questions. Select the letter that represents the BEST of the four possible choices.

THE CASE OF THE DELINQUENT TAXPAYER

David Owens has been a Tax Investigator for five years. His unit has received another anonymous tip about possible sales tax abuse, and David's supervisor, William, has assigned David to conduct the investigation. The organization in question is Bob's News, a 24-hour newsstand and variety store. The store is located in Hillsdell, five miles away. The anonymous caller did not provide details, but stated that she was an employee, and that there was widespread *abuse in the collection and reporting of sales tax by the store*. The agency has had a series of crank calls regarding sales tax abuse in Hillsdell.

For this investigation, David has been instructed not to work undercover, but to go in, identify himself, and discuss the situation with the owner and some employees without divulging the reason for the visit. On Wednesday, David drives to the store in a government car, a 1994 Plymouth.

David arrives at the store and buys a magazine for which he is properly not charged sales tax. He speaks to the employee whose name tag says Susan.

Hello, Susan, my name is David Owens, and I'm from the State Tax Department. Here's my identification. We're doing a routine check-up to see if things are in order with regard to sales tax collection and reporting. Is the owner around?

No, Bob is out of town today. He'll be back tomorrow. You seem surprised that his name is Bob. Some people think he must not exist, sort of like a Betty Crocker or something. Can I help you with anything? I'm the Assistant Manager.

Well, it would be helpful if you could answer a few questions for me.

As long as it doesn't get me in trouble with my boss, I'd be glad to, Susan replied.

Don't worry, I won't ask you anything that could get you in trouble.

OK, then.

Did someone tell employees how to go about collecting sales tax on items?

Bob has a list of items we're not allowed to collect tax on. It's right next to the cash register. Would you like to see it?

If you don't mind. Thanks. It says here not to collect tax on magazines, but there's no mention of newspapers.

I guess that's because he probably assumes we know better than that. I'll ask him to add it to the list.

This is a pretty good list, but what's this written on the bottom here about toilet paper? That's a taxable item.

Oh, I know. Henry who works nights put that in as a joke because he says toilet paper is a necessity, not a luxury, and shouldn't be taxed. I agree. So does Bob. But don't worry, we collect sales tax on it. Nine percent, right?

No, the rate is eight percent.

Just kidding, David. We know that. I guess I shouldn't joke about something like that; I don't want to end up in jail. What else do you need to know?

Who keeps the records and submits the sales tax money to Metro City every quarter?

Bob does that himself, but I'd rather you come back tomorrow to talk with him about that end of it....I think that would be best. I don't know much about it, except that he yells if I don't have everything - the records and stuff - ready for him when he wants it.

What time do you think Bob will be in tomorrow?

I think the morning would be best; you'll be sure to catch him then.

OK, I'll drop by tomorrow around nine. See you then. Thanks again.

The next day, David drives back to the store to meet with Bob at the time stated earlier. When he arrives, Susan immediately introduces him to Bob.

It's nice to meet you, Bob. Nice store you have here. How long have you been in business?

We've been open for five years. Time really flies, doesn't it?

It sure does. As Susan probably mentioned, I'm here on a routine type check-up about sales tax collection.

Sure thing.

Well, I just noticed you're not displaying the Sales Tax Certificate of Authority that you need to show in order to collect sales tax.

That's strange; it was there yesterday. Here it is. It fell under the counter. We're off to a great start. Let me tape this thing back up.

How many employees work here, Bob?

We have six full-time and three part-time employees, plus myself. I understand you'd like to see our books. Come on in to my office. Stay in here as long as you need. I've got it all laid out for you.

Thanks.

Several hours later, David finishes looking through the books.

Well, Bob, things look in order. The only question I have is why your receipts for 1994 were so much lower than in other years?

A chain store moved in about eight blocks away, and we initially lost a lot of business. But eventually our customers started coming back. We do the little things - save them the Boston papers, things like that. The chain moved downtown in early 1995.

Well, listen, thanks very much for all of your time. I really appreciate it.

No problem. Anytime. Well, I wouldn't go that far, but it's been nice meeting you.

1. What was the name of the Tax Investigator in the above passage? 1.___
   A. David Allen B. Bob Williams
   C. Derwin Williams D. David Owens

2. What was the name of the city the investigator visited? 2.___
   A. Hillsville B. Hillsdale
   C. Hicksville D. Hillsdell

3. The store under investigation is a 3.___
   A. department store
   B. 24-hour massage parlor
   C. newsstand and variety store
   D. sporting goods store

4. The phone call received by the agency was 4.___
   A. placed by an anonymous employee of the store being accused of sales tax fraud
   B. received by the investigator handling the case
   C. placed by an anonymous caller
   D. received by the investigator's supervisor

5. The investigator on this case 5.___
   A. did not work undercover
   B. was instructed to work undercover, but refused because of the nature of the case
   C. worked undercover
   D. pretended to his supervisor that he worked undercover

6. According to the above passage, it is 6.___
   A. not correct to charge sales tax for a magazine
   B. correct to charge sales tax for pet food
   C. correct to charge sales tax for a newspaper
   D. correct to charge sales tax for a magazine

7. The Assistant Manager of the store is 7.___
   A. Susan B. David
   C. Bob D. Betty Crocker

8. What day was the initial investigation conducted? 8.___
   A. Monday B. Wednesday
   C. Tuesday D. Thursday

9. The list the investigator was shown contained 9.___
   A. a list of sales taxable items
   B. a list of non-taxable items
   C. a list of products on which sales tax was mistakenly charged
   D. the Certificate of Authority

10. According to the above passage, sales tax was to be charged on 10.___
   A. pet food B. cigarettes
   C. gasoline D. toilet paper

11. According to the above passage, the sales tax was _____%. 11.___
A. seven B. nine C. eight D. ten

12. According to the passage, how often was the sales tax submitted? 12.___
A. Every month
B. Quarterly
C. Twice a year
D. Once every six months

13. According to the passage, where are the sales tax monies sent? 13.___
A. River City
B. Metro City
C. Metropolis
D. Hillswood

14. According to the passage, which of the following is TRUE? Bob's business, called Bob's 14.___
A. News and Variety, has been open for five years
B. Department Store, has been open for six years
C. Variety, has been open for six years
D. News, has been open for five years

15. The only question the investigator had about Bob's books was why receipts for _____ than in other years. 15.___
A. 1995 were so much lower
B. 1994 were so much lower
C. 1995 were so much higher
D. 1994 were so much higher

KEY (CORRECT ANSWERS)

1. D	6. A	11. C
2. D	7. A	12. B
3. C	8. B	13. B
4. C	9. B	14. D
5. A	10. D	15. B

REPORT WRITING

EXAMINATION SECTION

DIRECTIONS FOR THIS SECTION:
Each question or incomplete statement is followed by several suggested answers or completions. Select the one that *BEST* answers the question or completes the statement. *PRINT THE LETTER OF THE CORRECT ANSWER IN THE SPACE AT THE RIGHT.*

TEST 1

1. Following are six steps that should be taken in the course of report preparation: 1. ...
   I. Outlining the material for presentation in the report
   II. Analyzing and interpreting the facts
   III. Analyzing the problem
   IV. Reaching conclusions
   V. Writing, revising, and rewriting the final copy
   VI. Collecting data

   According to the principles of good report writing, the *CORRECT order* in which these steps should be taken is:
   A. VI, III, II, I, IV, V B. III, VI, II, IV, I, V
   C. III, VI, II, I, IV, V D. VI, II, III, IV, I, V
2. Following are three statements concerning written reports: 2. ...
   I. Clarity is generally more essential in oral reports than in written reports.
   II. Short sentences composed of simple words are generally preferred to complex sentences and difficult words.
   III. Abbreviations may be used whenever they are customary and will not distract the attention of the reader.

   Which of the following choices *CORRECTLY* classifies the above statements into whose which are valid and those which are not valid?
   A. I and II are valid, but III is not valid.
   B. I is valid, but II and III are not valid.
   C. II and III are valid, but I is not valid.
   D. III is valid, but I and II are not valid.
3. In order to produce a report written in a style that is both understandable and effective, an investigator should apply the principles of unit, coherence, and emphasis. 3. ...
   The *one* of the following which is the *BEST* example of the principle of coherence is
   A. interlinking sentences so that thoughts flow smoothly
   B. having each sentence express a single idea to facilitate comprehension
   C. arranging important points in prominent positions so they are not overlooked
   D. developing the main idea fully to insure complete consideration
4. Assume that a supervisor is preparing a report recommending that a standard work procedure be changed. Of the following, the *MOST* important information that he should include in this report is 4. ...
   A. a complete description of the present procedure
   B. the details and advantages of the recommended procedure
   C. the type and amount of retraining needed
   D. the percentage of men who favor the change

5. When you include in your report on an inspection some information which you have obtained from other individuals, it is *MOST* important that 5. ...
   A. this information have no bearing on the work these other people are performing
   B. you do not report as fact the opinions of other individuals
   C. you keep the source of the information confidential
   D. you do not tell the other individuals that their statements will be included in your report
6. Before turning in a report of an investigation of an accident, you discover some additional information you did not know about when you wrote the report. 6. ...
   Whether or not you re-write your report to include this additional information should depend *MAINLY* on the
   A. source of this additional information
   B. established policy covering the subject matter of the report
   C. length of the report and the time it would take you to re-write it
   D. bearing this additional information will have on the conclusions in the report
7. The *most desirable FIRST* step in the planning of a written report is to 7. ...
   A. ascertain what necessary information is readily available in the files
   B. outline the methods you will employ to get the necessary information
   C. determine the objectives and uses of the report
   D. estimate the time and cost required to complete the report
8. In writing a report, the practice of taking up the *least* important points *first* and the *most* important points *last* is a 8. ...
   A. *good* technique since the final points made in a report will make the greatest impression on the reader
   B. *good* technique since the material is presented in a more logical manner and will lead directly to the conclusions
   C. *poor* technique since the reader's time is wasted by having to review irrelevant information before finishing the report
   D. *poor* technique since it may cause the reader to lose interest in the report and arrive at incorrect conclusions about the report
9. *Which one* of the following serves as the *BEST* guideline for you to follow for effective written reports? Keep sentences 9. ...
   A. *short* and limit sentences to *one* thought
   B. *short* and use *as many* thoughts as possible
   C. *long* and limit sentences to *one* thought
   D. *long* and use *as many* thoughts as possible
10. One method by which a supervisor might prepare written reports to management is to begin with the conclusions, results, or summary, and to follow this with the supporting data. 10. ...

The *BEST* reason why management may *prefer* this form of report is that
A. management lacks the specific training to understand the data
B. the data completely supports the conclusions
C. time is saved by getting to the conclusions of the report first
D. the data contains all the information that is required for making the conclusions

11. When making written reports, it is *MOST* important that they be 11. ...
A. well-worded
B. accurate as to the facts
C. brief
D. submitted immediately

12. Of the following, the *MOST* important reason for a supervisor to prepare good written reports is that 12. ...
A. a supervisor is rated on the quality of his reports
B. decisions are often made on the basis of the reports
C. such reports take less time for superiors to review
D. such reports demonstrate efficiency of department operations

13. Of the following, the *BEST* test of a good report is whether it 13. ...
A. provides the information needed
B. shows the good sense of the writer
C. is prepared according to a proper format
D. is grammatical and neat

14. When a supervisor writes a report, he can *BEST* show that he has an understanding of the subject of the report by 14. ...
A. including necessary facts and omitting nonessential details
B. using statistical data
C. giving his conclusions but not the data on which they are based
D. using a technical vocabulary

15. Suppose you and another supervisor on the same level are assigned to work together on a report. You disagree strongly with one of the recommendations the other supervisor wants to include in the report but you cannot change his views. 15. ...
Of the following, it would be *BEST* that
A. you refuse to accept responsibility for the report
B. you ask that someone else be assigned to this project to replace you
C. each of you state his own ideas about this recommendation in the report
D. you give in to the other supervisor's opinion for the sake of harmony

16. Standardized forms are often provided for submitting reports. 16. ...
Of the following, the *MOST* important advantage of using standardized forms for reports is that
A. they take less time to prepare than individually written reports
B. the person making the report can omit information he considers unimportant

C. the responsibility for preparing these reports can be turned over to subordinates
D. necessary information is less likely to be omitted

17. A report which may *BEST* be classed as a *periodic* report is one which 17. ...
A. requires the same type of information at regular intervals
B. contains detailed information which is to be retained in permanent records
C. is prepared whenever a special situation occurs
D. lists information in graphic form

18. In the writing of reports or letters, the ideas presented in a paragraph are usually of unequal importance and require varying degrees of emphasis. 18. ...
All of the following are methods of placing extra stress on an idea *EXCEPT*
A. repeating it in a number of forms
B. placing it in the middle of the paragraph
C. placing it either at the beginning or at the end of the paragraph
D. underlining it

Questions 19-25.

DIRECTIONS: Questions 19 to 25 concern the subject of report writing and are based on the information and incidents described in the paragraph below. (In answering these questions, assume that the facts and incidents in the paragraph are true.)

On December 15, at 8 a.m., seven Laborers reported to Foreman Joseph Meehan in the Greenbranch Yard in Queens. Meehan instructed the men to load some 50-pound boxes of books on a truck for delivery to an agency building in Brooklyn. Meehan told the men that, because the boxes were rather heavy, two men should work together, helping each other lift and load each box. Since Michael Harper, one of the Laborers, was without a partner, Meehan helped him with the boxes for a while. When Meehan was called to the telephone in a nearby building, however, Harper decided to lift a box himself. He appeared able to lift the box, but, as he got the box halfway up, he cried out that he had a sharp pain in his back. Another Laborer, Jorge Ortiz, who was passing by, ran over to help Harper put the box down. Harper suddenly dropped the box, which fell on Ortiz' right foot. By this time Meehan had come out of the building. He immediately helped get the box off Ortiz' foot and had both men lie down. Meehan covered the men with blankets and called an ambulance, which arrived a half hour later. At the hospital, the doctor said that the X-ray results showed that Ortiz' right foot was broken in three places.

19. *What* would be the *BEST* term to use in a report describing the injury of Jorge Ortiz? 19. ...
A. Strain B. Fracture C. Hernia D. Hemorrhage

20. *Which* of the following would be the *MOST* accurate summary for the Foreman to put in his report of the incident? 20. ...
A. Ortiz attempted to help Harper carry a box which was too heavy for one person, but Harper dropped it before Ortiz got there.
B. Ortiz tried to help Harper carry a box but Harper got a pain in his back and accidentally dropped the box on Ortiz' foot.

C. Harper refused to follow Meehan's orders and lifted a box too heavy for him; he deliberately dropped it when Ortiz tried to help him carry it.
D. Harper lifted a box and felt a pain in his back; Ortiz tried to help Harper put the box down but Harper accidentally dropped it on Ortiz' foot.

21. One of the Laborers at the scene of the accident was asked his version of the incident. 21. ...
Which information obtained from this witness would be *LEAST* important for including in the accident report?
A. His opinion as to the cause of the accident
B. How much of the accident he saw
C. His personal opinion of the victims
D. His name and address

22. *What* should be the *MAIN* objective of writing a report about the incident described in the above paragraph? To 22. ...
A. describe the important elements in the accident situation
B. recommend that such Laborers as Ortiz be advised not to interfere in another's work unless given specific instructions
C. analyze the problems occurring when there are not enough workers to perform a certain task
D. illustrate the hazards involved in performing routine everyday tasks

23. *Which* of the following is information *missing* from the passage above but which *should be included* in a report of the incident? The 23. ...
A. name of the Laborer's immediate supervisor
B. contents of the boxes
C. time at which the accident occurred
D. object or action that caused the injury to Ortiz' foot

24. According to the description of the incident, the accident occurred *because* 24. ...
A. Ortiz attempted to help Harper who resisted his help
B. Harper failed to follow instructions given him by Meehan
C. Meehan was not supervising his men as closely as he should have
D. Harper was not strong enough to carry the box once he lifted it

25. *Which* of the following is *MOST* important for a foreman to *avoid* when writing up an official accident report? 25. ...
A. Using technical language to describe equipment involved in the accident
B. Putting in details which might later be judged unnecessary
C. Giving an opinion as to conditions that contributed to the accident
D. Recommending discipline for employees who, in his opinion, caused the accident

TEST 2

1. Lieutenant X is preparing a report to submit to his commanding officer in order to get approval of a plan of operation he has developed. 1. ...
The report starts off with the statement of the problem and continues with the details of the problem. It contains factual information gathered with the help of field and operational personnel. It contains a final conclusion and recommendation for action. The recommendation is supplemented by comments from other precinct staff members on how the recommendations will affect their areas of responsibility. The report also includes directives and general orders ready for the commanding officer's signature. In addition, it has two statements of objections presented by two precinct staff members.
Which one of the following, if any, is *either* an item that Lieutenant X *SHOULD HAVE INCLUDED* in his report and which is not mentioned above, *or* is an item which Lieutenant X *IMPROPERLY DID INCLUDE* in his report?
   A. Considerations of alternative courses of action and their consequences should have been covered in the report.
   B. The additions containing documented objections to the recommended course of action should not have been included as part of the report.
   C. A statement on the qualifications of Lieutenant X, which would support his expertness in the field under consideration, should have been included in the report.
   D. The directives and general orders should not have been prepared and included in the report until the commanding officer had approved the recommendations.
   E. None of the above, since Lieutenant X's report was both proper and complete.
2. During a visit to a section, the district supervisor criticizes the method being used by the assistant foreman to prepare a certain report and orders him to modify the method. This change ordered by the district supervisor is in direct conflict with the specific orders of the foreman. In this situation, it would be *BEST* for the assistant foreman to 2. ...
   A. change the method and tell the foreman about the change at the first opportunity
   B. change the method and rely on the district supervisor to notify the foreman
   C. report the matter to the foreman and delay the preparation of the report
   D. ask the district supervisor to discuss the matter with the foreman but use the old method for the time being
3. A department officer should realize that the *most usual* reason for writing a report is to 3. ...
   A. give orders and follow up their execution
   B. establish a permanent record
   C. raise questions D. supply information
4. A very important report which is being prepared by a department officer will soon be due on the desk of the district 4. ...

supervisor. No typing help is available at this time for the officer.
For the officer to write out this report in longhand in such a situation would be
  A. *bad;* such a report would not make the impression a typed report would
  B. *good;* it is important to get the report in on time
  C. *bad;* the district supervisor should not be required to read longhand reports
  D. *good;* it would call attention to the difficult conditions under which this section must work

5. In a well-written report, the length of each paragraph in the report should be 5. ...
  A. varied according to the content
  B. not over 300 words
  C. pretty nearly the same
  D. gradually longer as the report is developed and written

6. A clerk in the headquarters office complains to you about the way in which you are filling out a certain report. It would be *BEST* for you to 6. ...
  A. tell the clerk that you are following official procedures in filling out the report
  B. ask to be referred to the clerk's superior
  C. ask the clerk exactly what is wrong with the way in which you are filling out the report
  D. tell the clerk that you are following the directions of the district supervisor

7. The use of an outline to help in writing a report is 7. ...
  A. *desirable* in order to insure good organization and coverage
  B. *necessary* so it can be used as an introduction to the report itself
  C. *undesirable* since it acts as a straight jacket and may result in an unbalanced report
  D. *desirable* if you know your immediate supervisor reads reports with extreme care and attention

8. It is advisable that a department officer do his paper work and report writing as soon as he has completed an inspection *MAINLY* because 8. ...
  A. there are usually deadlines to be met
  B. it insures a steady work-flow
  C. he may not have time for this later
  D. the facts are then freshest in his mind

9. Before you turn in a report you have written of an investigation that you have made, you discover some additional information you didn't know about before. Whether or not you re-write your report to include this additional information should depend *MAINLY* on the 9. ...
  A. amount of time remaining before the report is due
  B. established policy of the department covering the subject matter of the report
  C. bearing this information will have on the conclusions of the report
  D. number of people who will eventually review the report

10. When a supervisoryofficer submits a periodic report to the district supervisor, he should realize that the *CHIEF* importance of such a report is that it 10. ...
    A. is the principal method of checking on the efficiency of the supervisor and his subordinates
    B. is something to which frequent reference will be made
    C. eliminates the need for any personal follow-up or inspection by higher echelons
    D. permits the district supervisor to exercise his functions of direction, supervision, and control better

11. Conclusions and recommendations are usually better placed at the *end* rather than at the *beginning* of a report because 11. ...
    A. the person preparing the report may decide to change some of the conclusions and recommendations before he reaches the end of the report
    B. they are the most important part of the report
    C. they can be judged better by the person to whom the report is sent after he reads the facts and investigations which come earlier in the report
    D. they can be referred to quickly when needed without reading the rest of the report

12. The use of the same method of record-keeping and reporting by *all* agency sections is 12. ...
    A. *desirable, MAINLY* because it saves time in section operations
    B. *undesirable, MAINLY* because it kills the initiative of the individual section foreman
    C. *desirable, MAINLY* because it will be easier for the administrator to evaluate and compare section operations
    D. *undesirable, MAINLY* because operations vary from section to section and uniform record-keeping and reporting is not appropriate

13. The *GREATEST* benefit the section officer will have from keeping complete and accurate records and reports of section operations is that 13. ...
    A. he will find it easier to run his section efficiently
    B. he will need less equipment
    B. he will need less manpower
    D. the section will run smoothly when he is out

14. You have prepared a report to your superior and are ready to send it forward. But on re-reading it, you think some parts are not clearly expressed and your superior may have difficulty getting your point. 14. ...
    Of the following, it would be *BEST* for you to
    A. give the report to one of your men to read, and if he has no trouble understanding it send it through
    B. forward the report and call your superior the next day to ask whether it was all right
    C. forward the report as is; higher echelons should be able to understand any report prepared by a section officer
    D. do the report over, re-writing the sections you are in doubt about

15. The *BEST* of the following statements concerning reports is that 15. ...
   A. a carelessly written report may give the reader an impression of inaccuracy
   B. correct grammar and English are unimportant if the main facts are given
   C. every man should be required to submit a daily work report
   D. the longer and more wordy a report is, the better it will read

16. In writing a report, the question of whether or not to include certain material could be determined *BEST* by considering the 16. ...
   A. amount of space the material will occupy in the report
   B. amount of time to be spent in gathering the material
   C. date of the material
   D. value of the material to the superior who will read the report

17. Suppose you are submitting a fairly long report to your superior. The *one* of the following sections that should come *FIRST* in this report is a 17. ...
   A. description of how you gathered material
   B. discussion of possible objections to your recommendations
   C. plan of how your recommendations can be put into practice
   D. statement of the problem dealt with

Questions 18-20.

DIRECTIONS: A foreman is asked to write a report on the incident described in the following passage. Answer Questions 18 through 20 based on the following information.

On March 10, Henry Moore, a laborer, was in the process of transferring some equipment from the machine shop to the third floor. He was using a dolly to perform this task and, as he was wheeling the material through the machine shop, laborer Bob Greene called to him. As Henry turned to respond to Bob, he jammed the dolly into Larry Mantell's leg, knocking Larry down in the process and causing the heavy drill that Larry was holding to fall on Larry's foot. Larry started rubbing his foot and then, infuriated, jumped up and punched Henry in the jaw. The force of the blow drove Henry's head back against the wall. Henry did not fight back; he appeared to be dazed. An ambulance was called to take Henry to the hospital, and the ambulance attendant told the foreman that it appeared likely that Henry had suffered a concussion. Larry's injuries consisted of some bruises, but he refused medical attention.

18. An *adequate* report of the above incident should give as minimum information the names of the persons involved, the names of the witnesses, the date and the time that each event took place, *and* the 18. ...
   A. names of the ambulance attendants
   B. names of all the employees working in the machine shop
   C. location where the accident occurred
   D. nature of the previous safety training each employee had been given

19. The *only one* of the following which is *NOT* a fact is 19. ...
   A. Bob called to Henry
   B. Larry suffered a concussion
   C. Larry rubbed his foot
   D. the incident took place in the machine shop

20. *Which* of the following would be the *MOST* accurate summary of the incident for the foreman to put in his report of the accident? 20. ...
   A. Larry Mantell punched Henry Moore because a drill fell on his foot and he was angry. Then Henry fell and suffered a concussion.
   B. Henry Moore accidentally jammed a dolly into Larry Mantell's foot, knocking Larry down. Larry punched Henry, pushing him into the wall and causing him to bang his head against the wall.
   C. Bob Greene called Henry Moore. A dolly then jammed into Larry Mantell and knocked him down. Larry punched Henry who tripped and suffered some bruises. An ambulance was called.
   D. A drill fell on Larry Mantell's foot. Larry jumped up suddenly and punched Henry Moore and pushed him into the wall. Henry may have suffered a concussion as a result of falling.

Questions 21-25.

DIRECTIONS: Answer Questions 21 through 25 *only* on the basis of the information provided in the following passage.

A written report is a communication of information from one person to another. It is an account of some matter especially investigated, however routine that matter may be. The ultimate basis of any good written report is facts, which become known through observation and verification. Good written reports may seem to be no more than general ideas and opinions. However, in such cases, the facts leading to these opinions were gathered, verified, and reported earlier, and the opinions are dependent upon these facts. Good style, proper form and emphasis cannot make a good written report out of unreliable information and bad judgment; but, on the other hand, solid investigation and brilliant thinking are not likely to become very useful until they are effectively communicated to others. If a person's work calls for written reports, then his work is often no better than his written reports.

21. Based on the information in the passage, it can be concluded that opinions expressed in a report should be 21. ...
   A. based on facts which are gathered and reported
   B. emphasized repeatedly when they result from a special investigation
   C. kept to a minimum
   D. separated from the body of the report

22. In the above passage, the *one* of the following which is mentioned as a way of establishing facts is 22. ...
   A. authority B. communication
   C. reporting D. verification

23. According to the passage, the characteristic shared by *all* written reports is that they are 23. ...
   A. accounts of routine matters
   B. transmissions of information
   C. reliable and logical D. written in proper form

24. *Which* of the following conclusions can *logically* be drawn from the information given in the passage? 24. ...
   A. Brilliant thinking can make up for unreliable information in a report.

B. One method of judging an individual's work is the quality of the written reports he is required to submit.
C. Proper form and emphasis can make a good report out of unreliable information.
D. Good written reports that seem to be no more than general ideas should be rewritten.

25. *Which* of the following suggested ittles would be *MOST* appropriate for this passage? 25. ...
A. Gathering and Organizing Facts
B. Techniques of Observation
C. Nature and Purpose of Reports
D. Reports and Opinions: Differences and Similarities

TEST 3

Questions 1-5.
DIRECTIONS: The following is an accident report similar to those used in departments for reporting accidents. Answer Questions 1 to 5 using *only* the information given in this report.

ACCIDENT REPORT

FROM *John Doe* DATE OF REPORT *June 23*
TITLE *Sanitation Man*
DATE OF ACCIDENT *June 22* TIME *3* AM PM
PLACE *1489 Third Avenue* CITY *Metropolitan*

VEHICLE NO. 1 (City Vehicle) VEHICLE NO. 2
OPERATOR *John Doe* *Sanitation Man* OPERATOR *Richard Roe*
Title ADDRESS *498 High Street*
VEHICLE CODE NO. *14-238* :LIC. NUMBER
LICENSE NO. *0123456* OWNER *Henry Roe* :
ADDRESS *786 E 83 St* : *5N1492*

DESCRIPTION OF ACCIDENT *Light green Chevrolet sedan while trying to pass drove into rear side of Sanitation truck which had stopped to collect garbage. No one was injured but there was property damage.*
NATURE OF DAMAGE TO PRIVATE VEHICLE *Right front fender crushed, bumper bent.*
DAMAGE TO CITY VEHICLE *Front of left rear fender pushed in. Paint scraped.*
NAME OF WITNESS *Frank Brown* ADDRESS *48 Kingsway*
John Doe BADGE NO. *428*
Signature of person making this report

1. Of the following, the *one* which has been omitted from this accident report is the 1. ...
A. location of the accident
B. drivers of the vehicles involved
C. traffic situation at the time of the accident
D. owners of the vehicles involved

2. The address of the driver of Vehicle No. 1 is not required because he 2. ...
A. is employed by the department
B. is not the owner of the vehicle
C. reported the accident D. was injured in the accident

3. The report indicates that the driver of Vehicle No. 2 was *probably* 3. ...
   A. passing on the wrong side of the truck
   B. not wearing his glasses
   C. not injured in the accident D. driving while intoxicated
4. The number of people *specifically* referred to in this report is 4. ...
   A. 3 B. 4 C. 5 D. 6
5. The license number of Vehicle No. 1 is 5. ...
   A. 428 B. 5N1492 C. 14-238 D. 0123456
6. In a report of unlawful entry into department premises, it is *LEAST* important to include the 6. ...
   A. estimated value of the property missing
   B. general description of the premises
   C. means used to get into the premises
   D. time and date of entry
7. In a report of an accident, it is *LEAST* important to include the 7. ...
   A. name of the insurance company of the person injured in the accident
   B. probable cause of the accident
   C. time and place of the accident
   D. names and addresses of all witnesses of the accident
8. Of the following, the *one* which is *NOT* required in the preparation of a weekly functional expense report is the 8. ...
   A. hourly distribution of the time by proper heading in accordance with the actual work performed
   B. signatures of officers not involved in the preparation of the report
   C. time records of the men who appear on the payroll of the respective locations
   D. time records of men working in other districts assigned to this location

---

KEYS (CORRECT ANSWERS)

TEST 1		TEST 2		TEST 3
1. B	11. B	1. A	11. C	1. C
2. C	12. B	2. A	12. C	2. A
3. A	13. A	3. D	13. A	3. C
4. B	14. A	4. B	14. D	4. B
5. B	15. C	5. A	15. A	5. D
6. D	16. D	6. C	16. D	6. B
7. C	17. A	7. A	17. D	7. A
8. D	18. B	8. D	18. C	8. B
9. A	19. B	9. C	19. B	
10. C	20. D	10. D	20. B	
	21. C		21. A	
	22. A		22. D	
	23. C		23. B	
	24. B		24. B	
	25. D		25. C	

PREPARING WRITTEN MATERIAL

PARAGRAPH REARRANGEMENT

COMMENTARY

The sentences which follow are in scrambled order. You are to rearrange them in proper order and indicate the letter choice containing the correct answer at the space at the right.

Each group of sentences in this section is actually a paragraph presented in scrambled order. Each sentence in the group has a place in that paragraph; no sentence is to be left out. You are to read each group of sentences and decide upon the best order in which to put the sentences so as to form as well-organized paragraph.

The questions in this section measure the ability to solve a problem when all the facts relevant to its solution are not given.

More specifically, certain positions of responsibility and authority require the employee to discover connections between events sometimes, apparently, unrelated. In order to do this, the employee will find it necessary to correctly infer that unspecified events have probably occurred or are likely to occur. This ability becomes especially important when action must be taken on incomplete information.

Accordingly, these questions require competitors to choose among several suggested alternatives, each of which presents a different sequential arrangement of the events. Competitors must choose the MOST logical of the suggested sequences.

In order to do so, they may be required to draw on general knowledge to infer missing concepts or events that are essential to sequencing the given events. Competitors should be careful to infer only what is essential to the sequence. The plausibility of the wrong alternatives will always require the inclusion of unlikely events or of additional chains of events which are NOT essential to sequencing the given events.

It's very important to remember that you are looking for the best of the four possible choices, and that the best choice of all may not even be one of the answers you're given to choose from.

There is no one right way to these problems. Many people have found it helpful to first write out the order of the sentences, as they would have arranged them, on their scrap paper before looking at the possible answers. If their optimum answer is there, this can save them some time. If it isn't, this method can still give insight into solving the problem. Others find it most helpful to just go through each of the possible choices, contrasting each as they go along. You should use whatever method feels comfortable, and works, for you.

While most of these types of questions are not that difficult, we've added a higher percentage of the difficult type, just to give you more practice. Usually there are only one or two questions on this section that contain such subtle distinctions that you're unable to answer confidently, and you then may find yourself stuck deciding between two possible choices, neither of which you're sure about.

EXAMINATION SECTION

DIRECTIONS: Each question consists of several sentences which can be arranged in a logical sequence. For each question, select the choice which places the numbered sentences in the MOST logical sequence. *PRINT THE LETTER OF THE CORRECT ANSWER IN THE SPACE AT THE RIGHT.*

1. I. A body was found in the woods. 1.___
II. A man proclaimed innocence.
III. The owner of a gun was located.
IV. A gun was traced.
V. The owner of a gun was questioned.

The CORRECT answer is:
A. IV, III, V, II, I
B. II, I, IV, III, V
C. I, IV, III, V, II
D. I, III, V, II, IV
E. I, II, IV, III, V

2. I. A man was in a hunting accident. 2.___
II. A man fell down a flight of steps.
III. A man lost his vision in one eye.
IV. A man broke his leg.
V. A man had to walk with a cane.

The CORRECT answer is:
A. II, IV, V, I, III
B. IV, V, I, III, II
C. III, I, IV, V, II
D. I, III, V, II, IV
E. I, III, II, IV, V

3. I. A man is offered a new job. 3.___
II. A woman is offered a new job.
III. A man works as a waiter.
IV. A woman works as a waitress.
V. A woman gives notice.

The CORRECT answer is:
A. IV, II, V, III, I
B. IV, II, V, I, III
C. II, IV, V, III, I
D. III, I, IV, II, V
E. IV, III, II, V, I

4. I. A train left the station late. 4.___
II. A man was late for work.
III. A man lost his job.
IV. Many people complained because the train was late.
V. There was a traffic jam.

The CORRECT answer is:
A. V, II, I, IV, III
B. V, I, IV, II, III
C. V, I, II, IV, III
D. I, V, IV, II, III
E. II, I, IV, V, III

5. I. The burden of proof as to each issue is determined before trial and remains upon the same party throughout the trial. 5.___
II. The jury is at liberty to believe one witness' testimony as against a number of contradictory witnesses.
III. In a civil case, the party bearing the burden of proof is required to prove his contention by a fair preponderance of the evidence.
IV. However, it must be noted that a fair preponderance of evidence does not necessarily mean a greater number of witnesses.
V. The burden of proof is the burden which rests upon one of the parties to an action to persuade the trier of the facts, generally the jury, that a proposition he asserts is true.
VI. If the evidence is equally balanced, or if it leaves the jury in such doubt as to be unable to decide the controversy either way, judgment must be given against the party upon whom the burden of proof rests.

The CORRECT answer is:
A. III, II, V, IV, I, VI
B. I, II, VI, V, III, IV
C. III, IV, V, I, II, VI
D. V, I, III, VI, IV, II
E. I, V, III, VI, IV, II

6. I. If a parent is without assets and is unemployed, he cannot be convicted of the crime of non-support of a child. 6.___
II. The term *sufficient ability* has been held to mean sufficient financial ability.
III. It does not matter if his unemployment is by choice or unavoidable circumstances.
IV. If he fails to take any steps at all, he may be liable to prosecution for endangering the welfare of a child.
V. Under the penal law, a parent is responsible for the support of his minor child only if the parent is *of sufficient ability*.
VI. An indigent parent may meet his obligation by borrowing money or by seeking aid under the provisions of the Social Welfare Law.

The CORRECT answer is:
A. VI, I, V, III, II, IV
B. I, III, V, II, IV, VI
C. V, II, I, III, VI, IV
D. I, VI, IV, V, II, III
E. II, V, I, III, VI, IV

7. I. Consider, for example, the case of a rabble rouser who urges a group of twenty people to go out and break the windows of a nearby factory. 7.___
II. Therefore, the law fills the indicated gap with the crime of *inciting to riot*.
III. A person is considered guilty of inciting to riot when he urges ten or more persons to engage in tumultuous and violent conduct of a kind likely to create public alarm.

IV. However, if he has not obtained the cooperation of at least four people, he cannot be charged with unlawful assembly.
V. The charge of inciting to riot was added to the law to cover types of conduct which cannot be classified as either the crime of *riot* or the crime of *unlawful assembly*.
VI. If he acquires the acquiescence of at least four of them, he is guilty of unlawful assembly even if the project does not materialize.

The CORRECT answer is:
A. III, V, I, VI, IV, II
B. V, I, IV, VI, II, III
C. III, IV, I, V, II, VI
D. V, I, IV, VI, III, II
E. V, III, I, VI, IV, II

8. I. If, however, the rebuttal evidence presents an issue of credibility, it is for the jury to determine whether the presumption has, in fact, been destroyed. 8.___
II. Once sufficient evidence to the contrary is introduced, the presumption disappears from the trial.
III. The effect of a presumption is to place the burden upon the adversary to come forward with evidence to rebut the presumption.
IV. When a presumption is overcome and ceases to exist in the case, the fact or facts which gave rise to the presumption still remain.
V. Whether a presumption has been overcome is ordinarily a question for the court.
VI. Such information may furnish a basis for a logical inference.

The CORRECT answer is:
A. IV, VI, II, V, I, III
B. III, II, V, I, IV, VI
C. V, III, VI, IV, II, I
D. V, IV, I, II, VI, III
E. II, III, V, I, IV, VI

9. I. An executive may answer a letter by writing his reply on the face of the letter itself instead of having a return letter typed. 9.___
II. This procedure is efficient because it saves the executive's time, the typist's time, and saves office file space.
III. Copying machines are used in small offices as well as large offices to save time and money in making brief replies to business letters.
IV. A copy is made on a copying machine to go into the company files, while the original is mailed back to the sender.

The CORRECT answer is:
A. I, II, IV, III
B. I, IV, II, III
C. III, I, IV, II
D. III, IV, II, I

10. I. Most organizations favor one of the types but always include the others to a lesser degree. 10.___
II. However, we can detect a definite trend toward greater use of symbolic control.
III. We suggest that our local police agencies are today primarily utilizing material control.
IV. Control can be classified into three types: physical, material, and symbolic.

The CORRECT answer is:
A. IV, II, III, I
B. II, I, IV, III
C. III, IV, II, I
D. IV, I, III, II

11. I. Project residents had first claim to this use, followed by surrounding neighborhood children. 11.___
II. By contrast, recreation space within the project's interior was found to be used more often by both groups.
III. Studies of the use of project grounds in many cities showed grounds left open for public use were neglected and unused, both by residents and by members of the surrounding community.
IV. Project residents had clearly laid claim to the play spaces, setting up and enforcing unwritten rules for use.
V. Each group, by experience, found their activities easily disrupted by other groups, and their claim to the use of space for recreation difficult to enforce.

The CORRECT answer is:
A. IV, V, I, II, III
B. V, II, IV, III, I
C. I, IV, III, II, V
D. III, V, II, IV, I

12. I. They do not consider the problems correctable within the existing subsidy formula and social policy of accepting all eligible applicants regardless of social behavior and lifestyle. 12.___
II. A recent survey, however, indicated that tenants believe these problems correctable by local housing authorities and management within the existing financial formula.
III. Many of the problems and complaints concerning public housing management and design have created resentment between the tenant and the landlord.
IV. This same survey indicated that administrators and managers do not agree with the tenants.

The CORRECT answer is:
A. II, I, III, IV
B. I, III, IV, II
C. III, II, IV, I
D. IV, II, I, III

13. I. In single-family residences, there is usually enough distance between tenants to prevent occupants from annoying one another. 13.___
II. For example, a certain small percentage of tenant families has one or more members addicted to alcohol.
III. While managers believe in the right of individuals to live as they choose, the manager becomes concerned when the pattern of living jeopardizes others' rights.
IV. Still others turn night into day, staging lusty entertainments which carry on into the hours when most tenants are trying to sleep.
V. In apartment buildings, however, tenants live so closely together that any misbehavior can result in unpleasant living conditions.
VI. Other families engage in violent argument.

The CORRECT answer is:
A. III, II, V, IV, VI, I B. I, V, II, VI, IV, III
C. II, V, IV, I, III, VI D. IV, II, V, VI, III, I

14. I. Congress made the commitment explicit in the Housing Act of 1949, establishing as a national goal the realization of *a decent home and suitable environment for every American family*. 14.___
II. The result has been that the goal of decent home and suitable environment is still as far distant as ever for the disadvantaged urban family.
III. In spite of this action by Congress, federal housing programs have continued to be fragmented and grossly underfunded.
IV. The passage of the National Housing Act signalled a new federal commitment to provide housing for the nation's citizens.

The CORRECT answer is:
A. I, IV, III, II B. IV, I, III, II
C. IV, I, II, III D. II, IV, I, III

15. I. The greater expense does not necessarily involve *exploitation*, but it is often perceived as exploitative and unfair by those who are aware of the price differences involved, but unaware of operating costs. 15.___
II. Ghetto residents believe they are *exploited* by local merchants, and evidence substantiates some of these beliefs.
III. However, stores in low-income areas were more likely to be small independents, which could not achieve the economies available to supermarket chains and were, therefore, more likely to charge higher prices, and the customers were more likely to buy smaller-sized packages which are more expensive per unit of measure.
IV. A study conducted in one city showed that distinctly higher prices were charged for goods sold in ghetto stores than in other areas.

The CORRECT answer is:

A. IV, II, I, III
B. IV, I, III, II
C. II, IV, III, I
D. II, III, IV, I

KEY (CORRECT ANSWERS)

1.	C	6.	C	11.	D
2.	E	7.	A	12.	C
3.	B	8.	B	13.	B
4.	D	9.	C	14.	B
5.	D	10.	D	15.	C

EXAMINATION SECTION

TEST 1

DIRECTIONS: Each question or incomplete statement is followed by several suggested answers or completions. Select the one that BEST answers the question or completes the statement. *PRINT THE LETTER OF THE CORRECT ANSWER IN THE SPACE AT THE RIGHT.*

1. Professional staff members in large organizations are sometimes frustrated by a lack of vital work-related information because of the failure of some middle-management supervisors to pass along unrestricted information from top management. 1.___
   All of the following are considered to be reasons for such failure to pass along information EXCEPT the supervisors'
   A. belief that information affecting procedures will be ignored unless they are present to supervise their subordinates
   B. fear that specific information will require explanation or justification
   C. inclination to regard the possession of information as a symbol of higher status
   D. tendency to treat information as private property

2. Increasingly in government, employees' records are being handled by automated data processing systems. However, employees frequently doubt a computer's ability to handle their records properly. 2.___
   Which of the following is the BEST way for management to overcome such doubts?
   A. Conduct a public relations campaign to explain the savings certain to result from the use of computers
   B. Use automated data processing equipment made by the firm which has the best repair facilities in the industry
   C. Maintain a clerical force to spot check on the accuracy of the computer's record-keeping
   D. Establish automated data processing systems that are objective, impartial, and take into account individual factors as far as possible

3. Some management experts question the usefulness of offering cash to individual employees for their suggestions. 3.___
   Which of the following reasons for opposing cash awards is MOST valid?
   A. Emphasis on individual gain deters cooperative effort.
   B. Money spent on evaluating suggestions may outweigh the value of the suggestions.
   C. Awards encourage employees to think about unusual methods of doing work.
   D. Suggestions too technical for ordinary evaluation are usually presented.

4. The use of outside consultants, rather than regular staff, in studying and recommending improvements in the operations of public agencies has been criticized. 4.___
Of the following, the BEST argument in favor of using regular staff is that such staff can better perform the work because they
   A. are more knowledgeable about operations and problems
   B. can more easily be organized into teams consisting of technical specialists
   C. may wish to gain additional professional experience
   D. will provide reports which will be more interesting to the public since they are more experienced

5. One approach to organizational problem-solving is to have all problem-solving authority centralized at the top of the organization. 5.___
However, from the viewpoint of providing maximum service to the public, this practice is UNWISE chiefly because it
   A. reduces the responsibility of the decision-makers
   B. produces delays
   C. reduces internal communications
   D. requires specialists

6. Research has shown that problem-solving efficiency is optimal when the motivation of the problem-solver is at a moderate rather than an extreme level. 6.___
Of the following, probably the CHIEF reason for this is that the problem-solver
   A. will cause confusion among his subordinates when his motivation is too high
   B. must avoid alternate solutions that tend to lead him up blind alleys
   C. can devote his attention to both the immediate problem as well as to other relevant problems in the general area
   D. must feel the need to solve the problem but not so urgently as to direct all his attention to the need and none to the means of solution

7. Don't be afraid to make mistakes. Many organizations are paralyzed from the fear of making mistakes. As a result, they don't do the things they should; they don't try new and different ideas. 7.___
For the effective supervisor, the MOST valid implication of this statement is that
   A. mistakes should not be encouraged, but there are some unavoidable risks in decision-making
   B. mistakes which stem from trying new and different ideas are usually not serious
   C. the possibility of doing things wrong is limited by one's organizational position
   D. the fear of making mistakes will prevent future errors

8. The duties of an employee under your supervision may be either routine, problem-solving, innovative, or creative. Which of the following BEST describes duties which are both innovative and creative? 8.___

A. Checking to make sure that work is done properly
B. Applying principles in a practical manner
C. Developing new and better methods of meeting goals
D. Working at two or more jobs at the same time

9. According to modern management theory, a supervisor who uses as little authority as possible and as much as is necessary would be considered to be using a mode that is 9.___
A. autocratic
B. inappropriate
C. participative
D. directive

10. Delegation involves establishing and maintaining effective working arrangements between a supervisor and the persons who report to him. 10.___
Delegation is MOST likely to have taken place when the
A. entire staff openly discusses common problems in order to reach solutions satisfactory to the supervisor
B. performance of specified work is entrusted to a capable person, and the expected results are mutually understood
C. persons assigned to properly accomplish work are carefully evaluated and given a chance to explain shortcomings
D. supervisor provides specific written instructions in order to prevent anxiety on the part of inexperienced persons

11. Supervisors often are not aware of the effect that their behavior has on their subordinates. 11.___
The one of the following training methods which would be BEST for changing such supervisory behavior is
A. essential skills training
B. off-the-job training
C. sensitivity training
D. developmental training

12. A supervisor, in his role as a trainer, may have to decide on the length and frequency of training sessions. 12.___
When the material to be taught is new, difficult, and lengthy, the trainer should be guided by the principle that for BEST results in such circumstances, sessions should be
A. longer, relatively fewer in number, and held on successive days
B. shorter, relatively greater in number, and spaced at intervals of several days
C. of average length, relatively fewer in number, and held at intermittent intervals
D. of random length and frequency, but spaced at fixed intervals

13. Employee training which is based on realistic simulation, sometimes known as "game play" or "role play," is sometimes preferable to learning from actual experience on the job. 13.___
Which of the following is NOT a correct statement concerning the value of simulation to trainees?

A. Simulation allows for practice in decision-making without any need for subsequent discussion.
B. Simulation is intrinsically motivating because it offers a variety of challenges.
C. Compared to other, more traditional training techniques, simulation is dynamic.
D. The simulation environment is nonpunitive as compared to real life.

14. Programmed instruction as a method of training has all of the following advantages EXCEPT: 14.___
A. Learning is accomplished in an optimum sequence of distinct steps
B. Trainees have wide latitude in deciding what is to be learned within each program
C. The trainee takes an active part in the learning process
D. The trainee receives immediate knowledge of the results of his response

15. In a work-study program, trainees were required to submit weekly written performance reports in order to insure that work assignments fulfilled the program objectives. 15.___
Such reports would also assist the administrator of the work-study program PRIMARILY to
A. eliminate personal counseling for the trainees
B. identify problems requiring prompt resolution
C. reduce the amount of clerical work for all concerned
D. estimate the rate at which budgeted funds are being expended

16. Which of the following would be MOST useful in order to avoid misunderstanding when preparing correspondence or reports? 16.___
A. Use vocabulary which is at an elementary level
B. Present each sentence as an individual paragraph
C. Have someone other than the writer read the material for clarity
D. Use general words which are open to interpretation

17. Which of the following supervisory methods would be MOST likely to train subordinates to give a prompt response to memoranda in an organizational setting where most transactions are informal? 17.___
A. Issue a written directive setting forth a schedule of strict deadlines
B. Let it be known, informally, that those who respond promptly will be rewarded
C. Follow up each memorandum by a personal inquiry regarding the receiver's reaction to it
D. Direct subordinates to furnish a precise explanation for ignoring memos

18. Conferences may fail for a number of reasons. Still, a conference that is an apparent failure may have some benefit. 18.___
Which of the following would LEAST likely be such a

benefit? It may

A. increase for most participants their possessiveness about information they have
B. produce a climate of good will and trust among many of the participants
C. provide most participants with an opportunity to learn things about the others
D. serve as a unifying force to keep most of the individuals functioning as a group

19. Assume that you have been assigned to study and suggest improvements in an operating unit of a delegate agency whose staff has become overwhelmed with problems, has had inadequate resources, and has become accustomed to things getting worse. The staff is indifferent to cooperating with you because they see no hope of improvement. 19.___
Which of the following steps would be LEAST useful in carrying out your assignment?

A. Encourage the entire staff to make suggestions to you for change
B. Inform the staff that management is somewhat dissatisfied with their performance
C. Let staff know that you are fully aware of their problems and stresses
D. Look for those problem areas where changes can be made quickly

20. Which of the following statements about employer-employee relations is NOT considered to be correct by leading managerial experts? 20.___

A. An important factor in good employer-employee relations is treating workers respectfully.
B. Employer-employee relations are profoundly influenced by the fundamentals of human nature.
C. Good employer-employee relations must stem from top management and reach downward.
D. Employee unions are usually a major obstacle to establishing good employer-employee relations.

21. In connection with labor relations, the term *management rights* GENERALLY refers to 21.___

A. a managerial review level in a grievance system
B. statutory prohibitions that bar monetary negotiations
C. the impact of collective bargaining on government
D. those subjects which management considers to be non-negotiable

22. Barriers may exist to the utilization of women in higher level positions. Some of these barriers are attitudinal in nature. 22.___
Which of the following is MOST clearly attitudinal in nature?

A. Advancement opportunities which are vertical in nature and thus require seniority
B. Experience which is inadequate or irrelevant to the needs of a dynamic and progressive organization

C. Inadequate means of early identification of employees with talent and potential for advancement
D. Lack of self-confidence on the part of some women concerning their ability to handle a higher position

23. Because a reader reacts to the meaning he associates with a word, we can never be sure what emotional impact a word may carry or how it may affect our readers. 23.___
The MOST logical implication of this statement for employees who correspond with members of the public is that
A. a writer should try to select a neutral word that will not bias his writing by its hidden emotional meaning
B. simple language should be used in writing letters denying requests so that readers are not upset by the denial
C. every writer should adopt a writing style which he finds natural and easy
D. whenever there is any doubt as to how a word is defined, the dictionary should be consulted

24. A public information program should be based on clear information about the nature of actual public knowledge and opinion. One way of learning about the views of the public is through the use of questionnaires. 24.___
Which of the following is of LEAST importance in designing a questionnaire?
A. A respondent should be asked for his name and address.
B. A respondent should be asked to choose from among several statements the one which expresses his views.
C. Questions should ask for responses in a form suitable for processing.
D. Questions should be stated in familiar language.

25. Assume that you have accepted an invitation to speak before an interested group about a problem. You have brought with you for distribution a number of booklets and other informational material. 25.___
Of the following, which would be the BEST way to use this material?
A. Distribute it before you begin talking so that the audience may read it at their leisure.
B. Distribute it during your talk to increase the likelihood that it will be read.
C. Hold it until the end of your talk, then announce that those who wish may take or examine the material.
D. Before starting the talk, leave it on a table in the back of the room so that people may pick it up as they enter.

KEY (CORRECT ANSWERS)

1. A	6. D	11. C	16. C	21. D
2. D	7. A	12. B	17. C	22. D
3. A	8. C	13. A	18. A	23. A
4. A	9. C	14. B	19. B	24. A
5. B	10. B	15. B	20. D	25. C

TEST 2

DIRECTIONS: Each question or incomplete statement is followed by several suggested answers or completions. Select the one that BEST answers the question or completes the statement. *PRINT THE LETTER OF THE CORRECT ANSWER IN THE SPACE AT THE RIGHT.*

1. Of the following, the FIRST step in planning an operation is to 1.___
   A. obtain relevant information
   B. identify the goal to be achieved
   C. consider possible alternatives
   D. make necessary assignments

2. A supervisor who is extremely busy performing routine tasks is MOST likely making INCORRECT use of what basic principle of supervision? 2.___
   A. Homogeneous Assignment
   B. Span of Control
   C. Work Distribution
   D. Delegation of Authority

3. Controls help supervisors to obtain information from which they can determine whether their staffs are achieving planned goals. 3.___
   Which one of the following would be LEAST useful as a control device?
   A. Employee diaries
   B. Organization charts
   C. Periodic inspections
   D. Progress charts

4. A certain employee has difficulty in effectively performing a particular portion of his routine assignments, but his overall productivity is average. 4.___
   As the direct supervisor of this individual, your BEST course of action would be to
   A. attempt to develop the man's capacity to execute the problematical facets of his assignments
   B. diversify the employee's work assignments in order to build up his confidence
   C. reassign the man to less difficult tasks
   D. request in a private conversation that the employee improve his work output

5. A supervisor who uses persuasion as a means of supervising a unit would GENERALLY also use which of the following practices to supervise his unit? 5.___
   A. Supervise and control the staff with an authoritative attitude to indicate that he is a "take-charge" individual
   B. Make significant changes in the organizational operations so as to improve job efficiency
   C. Remove major communication barriers between himself, subordinates, and management
   D. Supervise everyday operations while being mindful of the problems of his subordinates

6. Whenever a supervisor in charge of a unit delegates a routine task to a capable subordinate, he tells him exactly how to do it. 6.____
This practice is GENERALLY
   A. *desirable*, chiefly because good supervisors should be aware of the traits of their subordinates and delegate responsibilities to them accordingly
   B. *undesirable*, chiefly because only non-routine tasks should be delegated
   C. *desirable*, chiefly because a supervisor should frequently test the willingness of his subordinates to perform ordinary tasks
   D. *undesirable*, chiefly because a capable subordinate should usually be allowed to exercise his own discretion in doing a routine job

7. The one of the following activities through which a supervisor BEST demonstrates leadership ability is by 7.____
   A. arranging periodic staff meetings in order to keep his subordinates informed about professional developments in the field
   B. frequently issuing definite orders and directives which will lessen the need for subordinates to make decisions in handling any tasks assigned to them
   C. devoting the major part of his time to supervising subordinates so as to stimulate continuous improvement
   D. setting aside time for self-development and research so as to improve the skills, techniques, and procedures of his unit

8. The following three statements relate to the supervision of employees: 8.____
   I. The assignment of difficult tasks that offer a challenge is more conducive to good morale than the assignment of easy tasks
   II. The same general principles of supervision that apply to men are equally applicable to women
   III. The best retraining program should cover all phases of an employee's work in a general manner

Which of the following choices list ALL of the above statements that are generally correct?
   A. II, III
   B. I
   C. I, II
   D. I, II, III

9. Which of the following examples BEST illustrates the application of the "exception principle" as a supervisory technique? 9.____
   A. A complex job is divided among several employees who work simultaneously to complete the whole job in a shorter time.
   B. An employee is required to complete any task delegated to him to such an extent that nothing is left for the superior who delegated the task except to approve it.
   C. A superior delegates responsibility to a subordinate but retains authority to make the final decisions.
   D. A superior delegates all work possible to his subordinates and retains that which requires his personal attention or performance.

10. Assume that you are a supervisor. Your immediate superior frequently gives orders to your subordinates without your knowledge. 10.___
Of the following, the MOST direct and effective way for you to handle this problem is to
A. tell your subordinates to take orders only from you
B. submit a report to higher authority in which you cite specific instances
C. discuss it with your immediate superior
D. find out to what extent your authority and prestige as a supervisor have been affected

11. In an agency which has as its primary purpose the protection of the public against fraudulent business practices, which of the following would GENERALLY be considered an *auxiliary* or *staff* rather than a *line* function? 11.___
A. Interviewing victims of frauds and advising them about their legal remedies
B. Daily activities directed toward prevention of fraudulent business practices
C. Keeping records and statistics about business violations reported and corrected
D. Follow-up inspections by investigators after corrective action has been taken

12. A supervisor can MOST effectively reduce the spread of false rumors through the "grapevine" by 12.___
A. identifying and disciplining any subordinate responsible for initiating such rumors
B. keeping his subordinates informed as much as possible about matters affecting them
C. denying false rumors which might tend to lower staff morale and productivity
D. making sure confidential matters are kept secure from access by unauthorized employees

13. A supervisor has tried to learn about the background, education, and family relationships of his subordinates through observation, personal contact, and inspection of their personnel records. 13.___
These supervisory actions are GENERALLY
A. *inadvisable*, chiefly because they may lead to charges of favoritism
B. *advisable*, chiefly because they may make him more popular with his subordinates
C. *inadvisable*, chiefly because his efforts may be regarded as an invasion of privacy
D. *advisable*, chiefly because the information may enable him to develop better understanding of each of his subordinates

14. In an emergency situation, when action must be taken immediately, it is BEST for the supervisor to give orders in the form of 14.___
A. direct commands which are brief and precise
B. requests, so that his subordinates will not become alarmed

C. suggestions which offer alternative courses of action
D. implied directives, so that his subordinates may use their judgment in carrying them out

15. When demonstrating a new and complex procedure to a group of subordinates, it is ESSENTIAL that a supervisor 15.___
A. go slowly and repeat the steps involved at least once
B. show the employees common errors and the consequences of such errors
C. go through the process at the usual speed so that the employees can see the rate at which they should work
D. distribute summaries of the procedure during the demonstration and instruct his subordinates to refer to them afterwards

16. After a procedures manual has been written and distributed, 16.___
A. continuous maintenance work is necessary to keep the manual current
B. it is best to issue new manuals rather than make changes in the original manual
C. no changes should be necessary
D. only major changes should be considered

17. Of the following, the MOST important criterion of effective report writing is 17.___
A. eloquence of writing style
B. the use of technical language
C. to be brief and to the point
D. to cover all details

18. The use of electronic data processing 18.___
A. has proven unsuccessful in most organizations
B. has unquestionable advantages for all organizations
C. is unnecessary in most organizations
D. should be decided upon only after careful feasibility studies by individual organizations

19. The PRIMARY purpose of work measurement is to 19.___
A. design and install a wage incentive program
B. determine who should be promoted
C. establish a yardstick to determine extent of progress
D. set up a spirit of competition among employees

20. The action which is MOST effective in gaining acceptance of a study by the agency which is being studied is 20.___
A. a directive from the agency head to install a study based on recommendations included in a report
B. a lecture-type presentation following approval of the procedures
C. a written procedure in narrative form covering the proposed system with visual presentations and discussions
D. procedural charts showing the "before" situation, forms, steps, etc., to the employees affected

21. Which organization principle is MOST closely related to procedural analysis and improvement? 21.___
   A. Duplication, overlapping, and conflict should be eliminated.
   B. Managerial authority should be clearly defined.
   C. The objectives of the organization should be clearly defined.
   D. Top management should be freed of burdensome detail.

22. Which one of the following is the MAJOR objective of operational audits? 22.___
   A. Detecting fraud
   B. Determining organization problems
   C. Determining the number of personnel needed
   D. Recommending opportunities for improving operating and management practices

23. Of the following, the formalization of organization structure is BEST achieved by 23.___
   A. a narrative description of the plan of organization
   B. functional charts
   C. job descriptions together with organization charts
   D. multi-flow charts

24. Budget planning is MOST useful when it achieves 24.___
   A. cost control
   B. forecast of receipts
   C. performance review
   D. personnel reduction

25. GENERALLY, in applying the principle of delegation in dealing with subordinates, a supervisor 25.___
   A. allows his subordinates to set up work goals and to fix the limits within which they can work
   B. allows his subordinates to set up work goals and then gives detailed orders as to how they are to be achieved
   C. makes relatively few decisions by himself and frames his orders in broad, general terms
   D. provides externalized motivation for his subordinates

KEY (CORRECT ANSWERS)

1. B
2. D
3. B
4. A
5. D

6. D
7. C
8. C
9. D
10. C

11. C
12. B
13. D
14. A
15. A

16. A
17. C
18. D
19. C
20. C

21. A
22. D
23. C
24. A
25. C

POLICE SCIENCE NOTES

FORCE, SEARCH, AND SEIZURE

Use of Force

The right to use force against another varies according to the reasonable and apparent necessity that it be applied. The most important factors considered in the determination of how much force may be used by an officer are the following:

1. Is the force used or contemplated essential, or could the actor reasonably foresee that less force would be sufficient?
2. Does the crime to be prevented or the arrest to be attempted involve a felony or misdemeanor?
3. Does the act or crime to be prevented by force endanger property rights or human life and limb, and to what extent?
4. What are the responsibilities under law between the actor and what or whom he is attempting to protect with force?
5. Do departmental regulations restrict officers to less force than that permitted by statutes and court decisions?

When necessary, a police officer is permitted to use force in the performance of his duty to accomplish the following objectives:

1. To preserve the peace, prevent commission of offenses, or prevent suicide or self-inflicted injury.
2. To make *lawful* arrests and searches, to overcome resistance to such arrests and searches, and to prevent escapes from custody.
3. To defend himself or another against unlawful violence to his person or property.
4. To interrupt an intrusion on or interference with the lawful possession of property.

Lawful force is an aggressive act committed by a police officer in the performance of his duty when it is necessary to accomplish any of the objectives listed above. Deadly force is that which under the prevailing circumstances is capable of or intended to cause death or great bodily injury. Although lawful, or necessary, force is the *minimum* amount sufficient to achieve a legitimate police objective, this does not mean that an officer is permitted to escalate the force he uses without limit until the police objective is accomplished. For example, it would be illegal and immoral for an officer to use deadly force to prevent a person from unlawfully interfering with or even destroying another's personal property such as an automobile, even if under the circumstances, shooting the person would be the only way the destruction could be stopped.

Deadly force may be used to prevent a felony which threatens the life or safety of a person. However, when the felony does not involve such danger, the tendency of the law among jurisdictions to prohibit such extreme measures is steadily growing. Even in those jurisdictions in which the statutes and court cases continue to permit deadly force to be used to prevent felonies in which life is not endangered police departments are prohibiting it through their policies and regulations.

Once a crime has been committed the chief law enforcement interest is the apprehension of the offender. Although laws vary, deadly force may generally be used to effect the arrest of a dangerous criminal who is endangering or has threatened human life, but this amount of force may not be used on a thief no matter how much he stole. No jurisdiction punishes theft with the death penalty, so no officer should apply "capital punishment" to a thief.[1]

In no jurisdiction is deadly force permitted to effect an arrest for a misdemeanor. If the subject resists, the officer may escalate the amount of his force until it becomes deadly if this is necessary to protect himself from death or great bodily injury, and the officer is not required to retreat. However, the use of deadly force is not justified to apprehend a misdemeanant even though he is in flight and there is no other way to capture him.

The right of self-defense is based on the necessity of permitting a person who is attacked to take reasonable steps to prevent harm to himself. This right permits him

[1] It is still permissible in some jurisdictions to apply deadly force when necessary to effect the arrest of any felon, and some jurisdictions have even enacted such laws recently. See Florida Statutes §776.05, 051, 1975, Nevada Revised Statutes 200.140, 1975.

to use any reasonable force to prevent threatened harm, offensive bodily contact or confinement. Since it is a defense to a charge or accusation of use of force, the burden is on the actor to show the facts which caused him to use force and that it was reasonable.

The privilege to act to defend oneself arises not only when the danger is real but even when the danger does not in fact exist, providing that the belief in the presence and degree of danger is reasonable. For example, if, after a long, high speed, wild and reckless attempt on the part of a motorist to escape an officer the offender stops, leaps from his car and whips his hand inside his jacket, it would be reasonable for the officer to believe that he was about to be fired upon. It would be lawful use of deadly force for the officer to draw and fire his sidearm at the offender even if, in fact, the motorist was unarmed and reaching for only his wallet and driver license. The belief that he is threatened, however, must be that which a reasonable man would have under the circumstances. The person defending himself is not required to restrain himself with outstanding bravery, but on the other hand the reasonable man standard does not permit an abject coward to attack when there is no reasonable ground for his belief that he is in danger.

If force is continued after an attacker is disarmed, defeated, helpless, or the danger has passed, it is unlawful. No matter how gross the provovation had been on the part of the original attacker, there is no right to continue the use of force for revenge or punishment.

No officer should possess or use any weapon or incapacitating device which is neither issued nor approved by his department, including the ammunition in his firearm. Naturally, issued or approved weapons which have been materially altered to increase the force which they may apply should also not be possessed or used.

Under normal circumstances only the methods or weapons listed below should be used to apply force. It is the officer's responsibility to first exhaust every reasonable means of employing lesser force before escalating to a more severe application of force. The following methods are listed in ascending order from the least severe to the most drastic:

1. Physical strength and skill.
2. Approved noxious substance, mace, gas, etc.
3. Approved baton, sap, or blackjack.
4. Approved sidearm or other firearm loaded with approved ammunition.

Weapons should never be brandished or displayed as a threat unless their use under the circumstances would be reasonable and lawful.

Only those security devices or measures issued or approved by the department should be used to restrain those in custory, and the devices and measures should be used reasonably and only for the purpose of preventing:

1. Escape
2. Destruction of evidence
3. Attack
4. Self-inflicted injury
5. Commission of an offense

An officer who, out of anger or for the purpose of inflicting punishment or pain, cinches handcuffs too tightly, places a person in s straight jacket, strips a prisoner naked, puts an offender into a padded cell, incarcerates an offender with others who may attack him, or continues security measures when they are no longer reasonably necessary is acting unlawfully and reprehensibly.[2] It is the responsibility of the courts to punish, not the police.

The decision of an officer to use handcuffs or not is a difficult one. Opinions on this subject vary among experienced, professional officers. Where departmental regulations have been issued which state the circumstances under which handcuffs shall, may or must not be utilized they should be followed. However, because of the difficulty involved in covering all the possible situations in a regulation, they have not been written for officers' guidance in many agencies. The officer must then utilize his professional discretion.

The officer who decides whether or not to use handcuffs on the basis of his answer to, "If I were this prisoner, would I realize or could I be lead to understand that handcuffs are reasonable and necessary?" will arrive at the appropriate conclusion. An officer who states that "I handcuff everybody I arrest," does not, it is to be hoped, really do so. It is obviously ridiculous to handcuff "little ol' ladies" and small children without exception. On the other hand, the officer who fails to restrain dangerous felons, persons in a state of rage, or others who can be reasonably expected to do any of the acts which security measures are designed to prevent certainly should be handcuffed. An officer who fails to use his cuffs when it is appropriate endangers himself, his coworkers, the prisoner and others.[3]

Persons who are restrained by security devices are helpless, and officers must remain constantly aware of the possibility that such prisoners may be injured or suffer needlessly if precautions are not utilized. Therefore, secured persons must not be left unattended

[2] An officer who deliberately deprives a person of his constitutional rights violates 18 U.S.C. §242, a federal criminal statute. Intentional unnecessary violence has been held to deprive a prisoner of the right to due process before punishment. *United States v. Stokes*, 506 F.2d 771, 1975.

[3] Officers have been killed and injured by children of astonishingly tender ages. The ability to accurately determine from the circumstances, including nonverbal communications and body language, the inclinations of persons contacted is an important skill to be developed by every officer.

unnecessarily or otherwise subjected to needless danger or discomfort. The variety of possible situations to be avoided are too numerous to mention, but two must be. Prisoners should never be handcuffed to a vehicle which is used to transport them. If the vehicle is involved in an accident they cannot be removed from it if the officer is incapacitated or otherwise incapable of releasing them. It is appropriate to restrain handcuffed prisoners with safety belts because anybody can release the belts. However, if the person is handcuffed to the vehicle, only an officer can provide the key to the cuffs. Prisoners who indicate that they need to relieve themselves must be permitted to do so as soon as possible. The officer who refuses to permit his prisoner to use toilet facilities or to aid the nauseated person who must vomit is inflicting cruel and unusual punishment upon him.

Search and Seizure *

The most important factor relating to the law of search and seizure, and what each officer should seriously consider before he begins any search for or collection of evidence, is that WHENEVER POSSIBLE A SEARCH WARRANT SHOULD BE OBTAINED BEFORE SEARCHING FOR OR SEIZING EVIDENCE.

Both State and federal constitutions guarantee to everybody protection against unreasonable searches and seizures. This protection extends to their person, houses, papers and other property. No search warrant may be issued without probable cause, supported by oath or affirmation, and every warrant must particularly describe the place to be searched and the persons or things to be seized.[4]

The protection given by the Fourth Amendment arose from the unpleasant experiences suffered by colonial Americans when searches by English soldiers were conducted under the authority of "writs of assistance" or "general warrants." These writs and warrants were issued with little restraint, without probable cause, and empowered authorities to conduct searches virtually any place on the mere suspicion that goods subject to seizure might be discovered.

The words of the Fourth Amendment must be interpreted by the courts so that the meaning of the law can be applied to the fact situations of each case presented. Thousands of cases have defined "person," "houses," "probable cause," "search," and other words which appear in the Amendment.

Although persons subjected to unlawful searches and seizures have recourse to civil actions against officials who violate their rights,[5] the most common procedure by which they protect themselves is through the application of the exclusionary evidence rule. The exclusionary rule is simply that evidence obtained by unreasonable searches and seizures will not be admitted upon trial, usually upon objection raised by the defendant at a pre-trial "suppression hearing." The rule is not provided for in the Constitution, rather it was developed by the courts as their solution to the means by which the provision of the Amendment would be enforced. There are arguments both for and against the exclusionary rule, and many state courts did not adopt it. Today, however, it is universally applied in both federal and state courts because of the holding of the Supreme Court of the United Stated in the case of ***Mapp v. Ohio*** in 1961.[6] The purpose to be fulfilled by the rule is that officers will be deterred from illegally searching for or seizing evidence when they know that it cannot be used against the defendant to prove his guilt.[7]

Search Warrants

A search warrant is an order written in the name of the State, signed by a judicial officer in the proper exercise of his authority, directing a sheriff, constable, or other officer to search a specified place for evidence, stolen property or other "fruits" of a crime, or contraband, and to bring the articles enumerated before the court if they are discovered.

The following are criteria or requirements which must be met before a valid search warrant may be issued:

1. *Probable Cause*

If the facts in the affidavit are sufficient to lead a reasonable and prudent man to believe that a crime has been committed and that the articles described can be found at the place specified, then issuance of a search warrant is justified.[8] Information received by an officer from an undisclosed informant may be used as the basis for a search warrant, but the applicant for the warrant must be able to give the judicial officer substantial

*For a thorough discussion of current issues in search and seizure law see Israel, *Legislative Regulation of Searches and Seizures: The Michigan Proposals*, 73 Mich. L. Rev. 222 (1975).

[4] The Fourth Amendment to the Constitution reads: "The right of the people to be secure in their persons, houses, papers, and effects against unreasonable searches and seizures, shall not be violated, and no Warrants shall issue, but upon probable cause, supported by Oath or affirmation, and particularly describing the place to be searched, and the persons or things to be seized." The protection provided is both to the person, restricting arrests and detentions, and to his property, restricting searches for and seizures of things.

[5] 42 U.S.C. §1983 allows a civil suit for damages when a person acting under color of state law deprives another person of "any rights, privileges, or immunities secured by the Constitution and laws." See *Monroe v. Pope*, 365 U.S. 167, 1961.

[6] *Mapp v. Ohio*, 367 U.S. 643 (1961). The federal courts have operated under the exclusionary rule since *Weeks v. United States*, 232 U.S. 383 (1914).

[7] Other common law courts, such as the English, have not adopted the exclusionary rule.

[8] For an often quoted discussion of probable cause see *Brinegar v. United States*, 338 U.S. 160, 1949.

reasons to support the probable validity of the information which has been provided. The underlying circumstances upon which the applicant bases his belief must be specified by him. It is not sufficient to merely state, even with fervor, the police officer's belief. The facts of which he is aware which led to the development of that belief must also be stated.[9]

2. *Oath or Affirmation*

If this requirement is not fulfilled, the evidence obtained will not be admitted. The presumption that the magistrate had sworn the applicant is rebuttable by the defendant, and if no oath was administered the warrant is invalid and the evidence will be lost (excluded).

3. *Particular Description of Place and Things*

Whatever the wording to describe the place to be searched, the objective to be served is that the officers who are commanded to conduct the search will not, if they follow the description included in the warrant, search the wrong premises and disturb the rights of the innocent. If the warrant does not identify the property to be seized, it will not justify any seizure of that property. Contraband such as prohibited arms, explosive devices, and gambling equipment will ordinarily not be required to be as specifically described as stolen goods, since contraband is seizable by any officer lawfully observing it. When warrants are obtained for contraband the best description possible under the circumstances should always be attempted.

4. *Issuing Official*

The purpose served by requiring warrants is to assure that the innocent will not be disturbed by uncontrolled and unreasonable actions of officials of the executive branch of government. Therefore, the impartial and objective consideration by the judiciary of the probable cause and the reasonableness of the contemplated action is interposed as a restraint. Attempts to bypass this objective, even to accomplish other well founded purposes such as the efficient issuance of warrants, have generally been found unconstitutional by the courts.[10]

5. *Property Subject to Seizure*

Under early law, only stolen property could be seized under a search warrant. However, types of articles subject to seizure have been greatly expanded. Limitations still exist in some states such as requiring that only stolen or embezzled property (fruits of the crime), articles used to commit the crime (instrumentalities), or articles which are prohibited or controlled by statutes (contraband) may be seized. Such restrictions prevent officers from taking objects which are important as evidence, such as shoes worn by a suspect which could be compared with footprints found at the scene, but which fail to meet the definition of statutory restrictions. The United States Supreme Court in ***Warden v. Hayden*** held in 1967,[11] that statutes which permitted search warrants to issue for "mere evidence" are constitutional. It is up to those states which still follow the old rule to change their statutes or court decisions to permit seizure of evidence, but they are not required to do so.

Only those items specified in the warrant may be seized. If other property is seized it must be under authority other than that provided by the warrant.

6. *Execution Only By Those Ordered*

A search warrant may only be executed by those commanded by it to act, but the person designated may be specifically by either name or class (peace officers, for example). The person designated may be assisted by others, however.[12]

7. *Time Limit*

A search warrant must be executed within a reasonable time or it will fail to meet constitutional requirements. The amount of time which is reasonable varies, of course, according to the circumstances of each case. Most jurisdictions have by statute limited the time in which a search warrant may be executed, and the permissible period varies from a number of hours to more than a week. Some jurisdictions require special judicial authorization for warrants to be served at night.

8. *Prior Notice, Demand, and Forcible Entry*

If the local law allows and the warrant is for the seizure of items which can be destroyed quickly or if officers are aware of facts which reasonably lead them to believe notice to occupants would lead to danger of attack, entry may usually be effected without notice. Otherwise they are first required to notify persons within the premises of their identity and right to enter and make a demand that they be permitted to enter. Reasonable and necessary force may be used to effect entry when officers must act quickly to avoid evidence destruction or attack, or if they are denied entry after notice has been given and their demand had been refused. Force may also be used to enter unoccupied premises or when the denial is passive, for example, when occupants remain silent and do not open the door.

---

[9] The so-called Spinnelli-Aguilar rule was formulated in *Spinelli v. United States*, 394 U.S. 410, 1969, and *Aquilar v. Texas*, 378 U.S. 108, 1964.

[10] Efficiencies are clearly possible within this requirement. California and Arizona allow officers to secure search warrants by phonw, making it possible in some areas to get 65% of all warrants in under one hour and most of the rest within two hours. Miller, "Telephonic Search Warrants: The San Diego Experience," 9 *The Prosecutor* 385, 1974.

[11] 387 U.S. 294, 1967.

[12] Nonfederal officers should always be assisted by federal officers when serving a search warrant based on probable cause for a search relating to a strictly federal crime. *United States v. Townsend*, 394 F.Supp. 736, 1975.

Warrantless Searches and Seizures

Three factors have influenced and caused the development of those laws under which warrantless searches are permitted. They are permitted and lawful:

1. By consent
2. When necessity or emergency require immediate action
3. Where no right to protection exists

Consent Searches

A general principle of law is that one can waive any right or privilege to which he is entitled. However, because rights and privileges have arisen from previously experienced problems, courts observe very carefully the evidence presented in support of contentions that a defendant consented to a search.

Consent must be voluntary, the prosecution has the burden of proving consent clearly, and some sort of positive action by the person waiving must be shown.[13] For example, unless the person positively states his consent or makes some clearly understood gesture, the consent will not be held to be voluntary.

The search cannot extend beyond that granted by the terms of the consent in either area or time. That is, consent to search a room will not permit other rooms or the whole house to be searched, and the person may stop the search at any time simply by revoking his consent.[14]

The person consenting must have the capacity to do so. A person who has the right to possess premises or things may give consent, but others may not. For example, the occupant of a hotel room may consent to its search but not the management;[15] a parent can consent to a search of a minor child's room but not that of an adult child if the room is exclusively that child's, although permission to search areas used in common by the family is valid; a minor child's consent is unlikely to be held valid, but an adult child can consent to a search of at least jointly used areas; a spouse can consent if the premises are occupied by both spouses; and a person caring for the personal property of another may permit search of it.[16]

[13] See *Schneckloth v. Bustamonte*, 412 U.S. 218, 1973.

[14] Some states hold otherwise, that once given, consent cannot be withdrawn, but the trend of cases is that searches must stop immediately upon any revocation.

[15] *Stoner v. California*, 376 U.S. 483, 1964.

[16] *Frazier v. Cupp*, 394 U.S. 731, 1969.

Immediate Action Required

The most prevalent situations under which this exception is granted are searches made incident to a lawful arrest. Necessity is the motivating factor in permitting these searches. The two purposes served are to protect the arresting officer from attack and to prevent the person from access to things which would facilitate his escape, and to assure that evidence will not be destroyed by the defendant.[17]

Should any of the following criteria not be met the evidence discovered will be excluded:

1. The arrest must be lawful.
2. The search must be made for the purposes listed above (protection, security, evidence).
   * An arrest for an unlicensed vehicle, to be followed by a citation, may not be the basis for a search for drugs as there is no relationship between the offense and the purpose of the search.
3. The arrest must not be a sham or subterfuge made only to initiate a search not based on reasonable cause.[18]
   * An arrest warrant sworn out by officers (who merely suspect a burglary by the subject) charging the defendant with spitting on the sidewalk for the purpose of gaining entrance to his residence when they execute it—evidence of the burglary would be excluded.

Both the area searched and the time during which the search will be permitted are limited. Officers may make a reasonable search of areas within the person's reach or the distance through which he might be able to quickly leap in order to obtain a weapon for attack or evidence to destroy. Searching for evidence during an arrest beyond this area is no longer permitted without a search warrant.[19] The search must be made contemporaneously with the arrest. After the subject has been removed from the scene and/or confined in jail the

[17] *Chimel v. California*, 395 U.S. 752, 1969. Note that the same limitations on what types of articles (fruits of the crime, etc.) may be seized under a search warrant also apply in warrantless searches according to the law in the particular jurisdiction.

[18] Of course, if an officer can point to facts which, in the light of his experience, lead to the reasonable inference that the person whom he has stopped for a traffic offense is armed, he may search for the weapon to protect himself, *Terry v. Ohio*, 392 U.S. 88, 1968; but if he merely suspects that the person may be armed and *then* stops the person for a traffic violation as an excuse to search, the weapon will not be admissible.

[19] *Chimel v. California*, 395 U.S. 752, 1969, overruled the older rule allowing broader searches found in *Harris v. United States*, 331 U.S. 145, 1947, and *United States v. Rabinowitz*, 339 U.S. 56, 1960.

necessity of immediate action no longer prevails, and the officer must obtain a search warrant to search the area of the arrest.[20] An arrestee's person may be immediately fully searched, as opposed to a mere pat-down for weapons, incident to an arrest for which he is actually being taken into custody, or the search may be delayed until booking.[21] Once in jail, an arrestee or his property room effects may be researched without a warrant where the searches are not unreasonably made, i.e., harassment searches.[22]

The right of officers to search a car beyond the reach of the subject being arrested, for example in the closed trunk or even the locked glove compartment, would have to be based on grounds other than the arrest itself, i.e., on probable cause to search those areas, on consent, or "plain sight," or on a valid inventory.

When probable cause exists and the evidence is contained within a moving (or about to be moved) vehicle, officers may search.[23] There is a significant difference in the necessity for immediate action between searches of buildings and searches of vehicles which may speedily be moved out of the jurisdiction before a search warrant can be obtained. An occupied car on a highway is movable, and the persons within it are alerted to the presence of officers. The evidence may never again be located if courts were to require officers to obtain a warrant to search under these circumstances. To conduct a warrantless search of a "moving" vehicle, the officer should have that amount of information which would cause a court to readily issue a search warrant if there were time to procure one. The officer may make the search without first arresting the person. The search will be upheld under the vehicle exception if the essential requirements of probable cause are shown to have existed prior to the search.[24]

Where No Right to Protection Exists

Seizures of evidence without a search is not a violation of the Fourth Amendment when officers are lawfully present and the article seized is seen by them. Courts do not require officers to leave obvious evidence to be destroyed, but officers must not be trespassers at the time the evidence is observed. Furthermore, if an officer is a trespasser when he does see evidence, he cannot then procure a search warrant on the basis of the information he acquired as a trespasser.[25]

The protection offered by constitutional provisions are to protect persons against the acts of government officers, not private parties. Therefore, if a private person obtains evidence through unlawful entrance or burglary the evidence may be used against the criminal defendant. Of course, if an officer initiated the private person's action or participated in it, the evidence would be excluded. Searches and seizures are unlawful when they unreasonably intrude into areas where the person can reasonably expect privacy, but not outside those areas. Open fields, public streets and other places of similar description are outside the restrictions of the Fourth Amendment.[26]

Inventories of vehicles which come into the hands of the police through impounding procedures are permitted. The inventory made of the vehicle is for the purpose of making an inventory of its contents to protect the owner rather than a search for evidence of an offense. The officer's intrusion is only justifiable if it is a good faith attempt to protect the property in the car. In effect, the evidence is discovered "accidentally" while the officer is doing what he has a right to do and where he has legitimate cause to be.[27]

---

[20] *United States v. Davis*, 423 F.2d 974, 1970.

[21] *United States v. Robinson*, 414 U.S. 218, 1973, and *Gustafson v. Florida*, 414 U.S. 260, 1973. New York, California and Hawaii's State supreme courts have limited this recent expansion of police search freedom, however.

[22] *United States v. Edwards*, U.S. , 1974. Several states have more limited rules.

[23] *Texas v. White*, U.S. , 1975.

[24] *Carrol v. United States*, 267 U.S. 132, 1925; *Chambers v. Maroney*, 399 U.S. 42, 1970. If the car should more properly be considered to be a part of a household, for instance it is parked in a person's driveway, and there is no danger that it will be moved, a warrant is necessary. *Coolidge v. New Hampshire*, 403 U.S. 443, 1971.

[25] The "plain view" doctrine was discussed in *Coolidge v. New Hampshire*, 403 U.S. 443, 1971.

[26] The reasonable expectation of privacy analysis, discussed at length in *Katz v. United States*, 389 U.S. 347, 1967, greatly limits some uses of the "plain view" doctrine. For instance, police look in defendant's window from a fire escape. They are not trespassing, but may violate the defendant's reasonable expectation that no one would look in his window.

[27] *Cooper v. California*, 386 U.S. 58, 1967; *Harris v. United States*, 390 U.S. 234, 1968; *Cady v. Dombrowski*, 413 U.S. 1074, 1973.

PHILOSOPHY, PRINCIPLES, PRACTICES, AND TECHNICS
OF
SUPERVISION, ADMINISTRATION, MANAGEMENT, AND ORGANIZATION

CONTENTS

CONTENTS (cont'd)

PHILOSOPHY, PRINCIPLES, PRACTICES, AND TECHNICS OF SUPERVISION, ADMINISTRATION, MANAGEMENT, AND ORGANIZATION

I. MEANING OF SUPERVISION

The extension of the democratic philosophy has been accompanied by an extension in the scope of supervision. Modern leaders and supervisors no longer think of supervision in the narrow sense of being confined chiefly to visiting employees, supplying materials, or rating the staff. They regard supervision as being intimately related to all the concerned agencies of society, they speak of the supervisor's function in terms of "growth", rather than the "improvement," of employees

This modern concept of supervision may be defined as follows:

Supervision is leadership and the development of leadership within groups which are cooperatively engaged in inspection, research, training, guidance and evaluation.

II. THE OLD AND THE NEW SUPERVISION

TRADITIONAL	*MODERN*
1. Inspection	1. Study and analysis
2. Focused on the employee	2. Focused on aims, materials, methods, supervisors, employees, environment
3. Visitation	3. Demonstrations, intervisitation, workshops, directed reading, bulletins, etc.
4. Random and haphazard	4. Definitely organized and planned (scientific)
5. Imposed and authoritarian	5. Cooperative and democratic
6. One person usually	6. Many persons involved (creative)

III. THE EIGHT (8) BASIC PRINCIPLES OF THE NEW SUPERVISION

1. *PRINCIPLE OF RESPONSIBILITY*

   Authority to act and responsibility for acting must be joined.

   a. If you give responsibility, give authority.
   b. Define employee duties clearly.
   c. Protect employees from criticism by others.
   d. Recognize the rights as well as obligations of employees.
   e. Achieve the aims of a democratic society insofar as it is possible within the area of your work.
   f. Establish a situation favorable to training and learning.
   g. Accept ultimate responsibility for everything done in your section, unit, office, division, department.
   h. Good administration and good supervision are inseparable.

2. *PRINCIPLE OF AUTHORITY*

   The success of the supervisor is measured by the extent to which the power of authority is not used.

   a. Exercise simplicity and informality in supervision.
   b. Use the simplest machinery of supervision.
   c. If it is good for the organization as a whole, it is probably justified.
   d. Seldom be arbitrary or authoritative.
   e. Do not base your work on the power of position or of personality.
   f. Permit and encourage the free expression of opinions.

3. *PRINCIPLE OF SELF-GROWTH*

   The success of the supervisor is measured by the extent to which, and the speed with which, he is no longer needed.

   a. Base criticism on principles, not on specifics.
   b. Point out higher activities to employees.

c. Train for self-thinking by employees, to meet new situations.
d. Stimulate initiative, self-reliance and individual responsibility.
e. Concentrate on stimulating the growth of employees rather than on removing defects.

4. *PRINCIPLE OF INDIVIDUAL WORTH*

Respect for the individual is a paramount consideration in supervision.

a. Be human and sympathetic in dealing with employees.
b. Don't nag about things to be done.
c. Recognize the individual differences among employees and seek opportunities to permit best expression of each personality.

5. *PRINCIPLE OF CREATIVE LEADERSHIP*

The best supervision is that which is not apparent to the employee.

a. Stimulate, don't drive employees to creative action.
b. Emphasize doing good things.
c. Encourage employees to do what they do best.
d. Do not be too greatly concerned with details of subject or method.
e. Do not be concerned exclusively with immediate problems and activities.
f. Reveal higher activities and make them both desired and maximally possible.
g. Determine procedures in the light of each situation but see that these are derived from a sound basic philosophy.
h. Aid, inspire and lead so as to liberate the creative spirit latent in all good employees.

6. *PRINCIPLE OF SUCCESS AND FAILURE*

There are no unsuccessful employees, only unsuccessful supervisors who have failed to give proper leadership.

a. Adapt suggestions to the capacities, attitudes, and prejudices of employees.
b. Be gradual, be progressive, be persistent.
c. Help the employee find the general principle; have the employee apply his own problem to the general principle.
d. Give adequate appreciation for good work and honest effort.
e. Anticipate employee difficulties and help to prevent them.
f. Encourage employees to do the desirable things they will do anyway.
g. Judge your supervision by the results it secures.

7. *PRINCIPLE OF SCIENCE*

Successful supervision is scientific, objective, and experimental. It is based on facts, not on prejudices.

a. Be cumulative in results.
b. Never divorce your suggestions from the goals of training.
c. Don't be impatient of results.
d. Keep all matters on a professional, not a personal level.
e. Do not be concerned exclusively with immediate problems and activities.
f. Use objective means of determining achievement and rating where possible.

8. *PRINCIPLE OF COOPERATION*

Supervision is a cooperative enterprise between supervisor and employee.

a. Begin with conditions as they are.
b. Ask opinions of all involved when formulating policies.

c. Organization is as good as its weakest link.
d. Let employees help to determine policies and department programs.
e. Be approachable and accessible - physically and mentally.
f. Develop pleasant social relationships.

IV. WHAT IS ADMINISTRATION?

Administration is concerned with providing the environment, the material facilities,and the operational procedures that will promote the maximum growth and development of supervisors and employees. (Organization is an aspect,and a concomitant,of administration.)

There is no sharp line of demarcation between supervision and administration; these functions are intimately interrelated and,often, overlapping. They are complementary activities.

1. *PRACTICES COMMONLY CLASSED AS "SUPERVISORY"*
   a. Conducting employees conferences
   b. Visiting sections,units,offices,divisions,departments
   c. Arranging for demonstrations
   d. Examining plans
   e. Suggesting professional reading
   f. Interpreting bulletins
   g. Recommending in-service training courses
   h. Encouraging experimentation
   i. Appraising employee morale
   j. Providing for intervisitation
2. *PRACTICES COMMONLY CLASSIFIED AS "ADMINISTRATIVE"*
   a. Management of the office
   b. Arrangement of schedules for extra duties
   c. Assignment of rooms or areas
   d. Distribution of supplies
   e. Keeping records and reports
   f. Care of audio-visual materials
   g. Keeping inventory records
   h. Checking record cards and books
   i. Programming special activities
   j. Checking on the attendance and punctuality of employees
3. *PRACTICES COMMONLY CLASSIFIED AS BOTH "SUPERVISORY" AND "ADMINISTRATIVE"*
   a. Program construction
   b. Testing or evaluating outcomes
   c. Personnel accounting
   d. Ordering instructional materials

V. RESPONSIBILITIES OF THE SUPERVISOR

A person employed in a supervisory capacity must constantly be able to improve his own efficiency and ability. He represents the employer to the employees and only continuous self-examination can make him a capable supervisor.

Leadership and training are the supervisor's responsibility. An efficient working unit is one in which the employees work with the supervisor. It is his job to bring out the best in his employees. He must always be relaxed,courteous and calm in his association with his employees. Their feelings are important, and a harsh attitude does not develop the most efficient employees.

VI. COMPETENCIES OF THE SUPERVISOR

1. Complete knowledge of the duties and responsibilities of his position.
2. To be able to organize a job, plan ahead and carry through.
3. To have self-confidence and initiative.
4. To be able to handle the unexpected situation and make quick decisions.
5. To be able to properly train subordinates in the positions they are best suited for.
6. To be able to keep good human relations among his subordinates.
7. To be able to keep good human relations between his subordinates and himself and to earn their respect and trust.

VII. THE PROFESSIONAL SUPERVISOR-EMPLOYEE RELATIONSHIP

There are two kinds of efficiency: one kind is only apparent and is produced in organizations through the exercise of mere discipline; this is but a simulation of the second, or true, efficiency which springs from spontaneous cooperation. If you are a manager, no matter how great or small your responsibility, it is your job, in the final analysis, to create and develop this involuntary cooperation among the people whom you supervise. For, no matter how powerful a combination of money, machines, and materials a company may have, this is a dead and sterile thing without a team of willing, thinking and articulate people to guide it.

The following 21 points are presented as indicative of the exemplary basic relationship that should exist between supervisor and employee:

1. Each person wants to be liked and respected by his fellow employee and wants to be treated with consideration and respect by his superior.
2. The most competent employee will make an error. However, in a unit where good relations exist between the supervisor and his employees, tenseness and fear do not exist. Thus, errors are not hidden or covered up and the efficiency of a unit is not impaired.
3. Subordinates resent rules, regulations, or orders that are unreasonable or unexplained.
4. Subordinates are quick to resent unfairness, harshness, injustices and favoritism.
5. An employee will accept responsibility if he knows that he will be complimented for a job well done, and not too harshly chastized for failure; that his supervisor will check the cause of the failure, and, if it was the supervisor's fault, he will assume the blame therefor. If it was the employee's fault, his supervisor will explain the correct method or means of handling the responsibility.
6. An employee wants to receive credit for a suggestion he has made, that is used. If a suggestion cannot be used, the employee is entitled to an explanation. The supervisor should not say "no" and close the subject.
7. Fear and worry slow up a worker's ability. Poor working environment can impair his physical and mental health. A good supervisor avoids forceful methods, threats and arguments to get a job done.
8. A forceful supervisor is able to train his employees individually and as a team, and is able to motivate them in the proper channels.

9. A mature supervisor is able to properly evaluate his subordinates and to keep them happy and satisfied.
10. A sensitive supervisor will never patronize his subordinates.
11. A worthy supervisor will respect his employees' confidences.
12. Definite and clear-cut responsibilities should be assigned to each executive.
13. Responsibility should always be coupled with corresponding authority.
14. No change should be made in the scope or responsibilities of a position without a definite understanding to that effect on the part of all persons concerned.
15. No executive or employee, occupying a single position in the organization, should be subject to definite orders from more than one source.
16. Orders should never be given to subordinates over the head of a responsible executive. Rather than do this, the officer in question should be supplanted.
17. Criticisms of subordinates should, whever possible, be made privately, and in no case should a subordinate be criticized in the presence of executives or employees of equal or lower rank.
18. No dispute or difference between executives or employees as to authority or responsibilities should be considered too trivial for prompt and careful adjudication.
19. Promotions, wage changes, and disciplinary action should always be approved by the executive immediately superior to the one directly responsible.
20. No executive or employee should ever be required, or expected, to be at the same time an assistant to, and critic of, another.
21. Any executive whose work is subject to regular inspection should, whever practicable, be given the assistance and facilities necessary to enable him to maintain an independent check of the quality of his work.

VIII. MINI-TEXT IN SUPERVISION, ADMINISTRATION, MANAGEMENT, AND ORGANIZATION

A. BRIEF HIGHLIGHTS

Listed concisely and sequentially are major headings and important data in the field for quick recall and review.

1. *LEVELS OF MANAGEMENT*

Any organization of some size has several levels of management. In terms of a ladder the levels are:

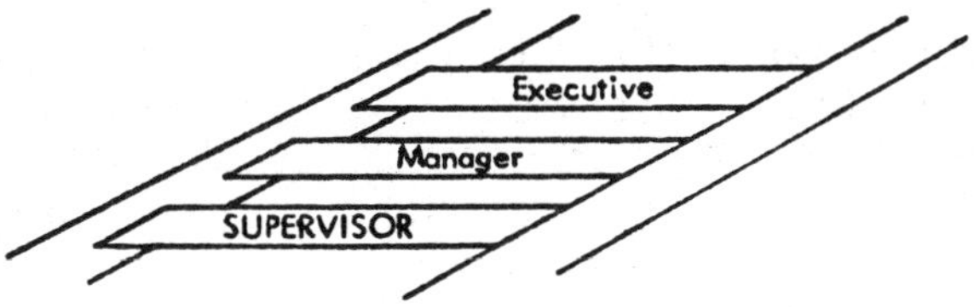

The first level is very important because it is the beginning point of management leadership.

2. *WHAT THE SUPERVISOR MUST LEARN*

A supervisor must learn to:

(1) Deal with people and their differences
(2) Get the job done through people
(3) Recognize the problems when they exist
(4) Overcome obstacles to good performance
(5) Evaluate the performance of people
(6) Check his own performance in terms of accomplishment

3. *A DEFINITION OF SUPERVISOR*

The term supervisor means any individual having authority, in the interests of the employer, to hire, transfer, suspend, lay-off, recall, promote, discharge, assign, reward, or discipline other employees... or responsibility to direct them, or to adjust their grievances, or effectively to recommend such action, if, in connection with the foregoing, exercise of such authority is not of a merely routine or clerical nature but requires the use of independent judgment.

4. *ELEMENTS OF THE TEAM CONCEPT*

What is involved in teamwork? The component parts are:

(1) Members
(2) A leader
(3) Goals
(4) Plans
(5) Cooperation
(6) Spirit

5. *PRINCIPLES OF ORGANIZATION*

(1) A team member must know what his job is
(2) Be sure that the nature and scope of a job are understood
(3) Authority and responsibility should be carefully spelled out
(4) A supervisor should be permitted to make the maximum number of decisions affecting his employees
(5) Employees should report to only one supervisor
(6) A supervisor should direct only as many employees as he can handle effectively
(7) An organization plan should be flexible
(8) Inspection and performance of work should be separate
(9) Organizational problems should receive immediate attention
(10) Assign work in line with ability and experience

6. *THE FOUR IMPORTANT PARTS OF EVERY JOB*

(1) Inherent in every job is the *accountability* for results
(2) A second set of factors in every job are *responsibilities*
(3) Along with duties and responsibilities one must have the *authority* to act within certain limits without obtaining permission to proceed
(4) No job exists in a vacuum. The supervisor is surrounded by key *relationships*

7. *PRINCIPLES OF DELEGATION*

Where work is delegated for the first time, the supervisor should think in terms of these questions:

(1) Who is best qualified to do this?
(2) Can an employee improve his abilities by doing this?
(3) How long should an employee spend on this?
(4) Are there any special problems for which he will need guidance?
(5) How broad a delegation can I make?

8. *PRINCIPLES OF EFFECTIVE COMMUNICATIONS*

(1) Determine the media
(2) To whom directed?
(3) Identification and source authority
(4) Is communication understood?

9. *PRINCIPLES OF WORK IMPROVEMENT*

(1) Most people usually do only the work which is assigned to them
(2) Workers are likely to fit assigned work into the time available to perform it
(3) A good workload usually stimulates output
(4) People usually do their best work when they know that results will be reviewed or inspected

(5) Employees usually feel that someone else is responsible for conditions of work, workplace layout, job methods, type of tools and equipment, and other such factors
(6) Employees are usually defensive about their job security
(7) Employees have natural resistance to change
(8) Employees can support or destroy a supervisor
(9) A supervisor usually earns the respect of his people through his personal example of diligence and efficiency

10. *AREAS OF JOB IMPROVEMENT*

The *areas* of job improvement are quite numerous, but the most common ones which a supervisor can identify and utilize are:

(1) Departmental layout
(2) Flow of work
(3) Workplace layout
(4) Utilization of manpower
(5) Work methods
(6) Materials handling
(7) Utilization
(8) Motion economy

11. *SEVEN KEY POINTS IN MAKING IMPROVEMENTS*

(1) Select the job to be improved
(2) Study how it is being done now
(3) Question the present method
(4) Determine actions to be taken
(5) Chart proposed method
(6) Get approval and apply
(7) Solicit worker participation

12. *CORRECTIVE TECHNIQUES OF JOB IMPROVEMENT*

Specific Problems	*General Problems*	*Corrective Technique*
(1) Size of workload	(1) Departmental layout	(1) Study with scale model
(2) Inability to meet schedules	(2) Flow of work	(2) Flow chart study
(3) Strain and fatigue	(3) Workplan layout	(3) Motion analysis
(4) Improper use of men and skills	(4) Utilization of manpower	(4) Comparison of units produced to standard allowances
(5) Waste, poor quality, unsafe conditions	(5) Work methods	(5) Methods analysis
(6) Bottleneck conditions that hinder output	(6) Materials handling	(6) Flow chart and equipment study
(7) Poor utilization of equipment and machines	(7) Utilization of equipment	(7) Down time vs. running time
(8) Efficiency and productivity of labor	(8) Motion economy	(8) Motion analysis

13. *A PLANNING CHECKLIST*

(1) Objectives
(2) Controls
(3) Delegations
(4) Communications
(5) Resources
(6) Methods and procedures
(7) Manpower
(8) Equipment
(9) Supplies and materials
(10) Utilization of time
(11) Safety
(12) Money
(13) Work
(14) Timing of improvements

14. *FIVE CHARACTERISTICS OF GOOD DIRECTIONS*

In order to get results, directions must be:

(1) Possible of accomplishment
(2) Agreeable with worker interests
(3) Related to mission
(4) Planned and complete
(5) Unmistakably clear

15. *TYPES OF DIRECTIONS*
    (1) Demands or direct orders
    (2) Requests
    (3) Suggestion or implication
    (4) Volunteering

16. *CONTROLS*

A typical listing of the overall areas in which the supervisor should establish controls might be:
    (1) Manpower
    (2) Materials
    (3) Quality of work
    (4) Quantity of work
    (5) Time
    (6) Space
    (7) Money
    (8) Methods

17. *ORIENTING THE NEW EMPLOYEE*
    (1) Prepare for him
    (2) Welcome the new employee
    (3) Orientation for the job
    (4) Follow-up

18. *CHECKLIST FOR ORIENTING NEW EMPLOYEES*

	Yes	*No*
(1) Do your appreciate the feelings of new employees when they first report for work?	...	...
(2) Are you aware of the fact that the new employee must make a big adjustment to his job?	...	...
(3) Have you given him good reasons for liking the job and the organization?	...	...
(4) Have you prepared for his first day on the job?	...	...
(5) Did you welcome him cordially and make him feel needed?	...	...
(6) Did you establish rapport with him so that he feels free to talk and discuss matters with you?	...	...
(7) Did you explain his job to him and his relationship to you?	...	...
(8) Does he know that his work will be evaluated periodically on a basis that is fair and objective?	..	...
(9) Did you introduce him to his fellow workers in such a way that they are likely to accept him?	...	...
(10) Does he know what employee benefits he will receive?	...	...
(11) Does he understand the importance of being on the job and what to do if he must leave his duty station?	...	...
(12) Has he been impressed with the importance of accident prevention and safe practice?	...	...
(13) Does he generally know his way around the department?	...	...
(14) Is he under the guidance of a sponsor who will teach the right ways of doing things?	...	...
(15) Do you plan to follow-up so that he will continue to adjust successfully to his job?	...	...

19. *PRINCIPLES OF LEARNING*
    (1) Motivation
    (2) Demonstration or explanation
    (3) Practice

20. *CAUSES OF POOR PERFORMANCE*
    (1) Improper training for job
    (2) Wrong tools
    (3) Inadequate directions
    (4) Lack of supervisory follow-up
    (5) Poor communications
    (6) Lack of standards of performance
    (7) Wrong work habits
    (8) Low morale
    (9) Other

21. *FOUR MAJOR STEPS IN ON-THE-JOB INSTRUCTION*
    (1) Prepare the worker
    (2) Present the operation
    (3) Tryout performance
    (4) Follow-up

22. *EMPLOYEES WANT FIVE THINGS*
(1) Security (2) Opportunity (3) Recognition
(4) Inclusion (5) Expression

23. *SOME DON'TS IN REGARD TO PRAISE*
(1) Don't praise a person for something he hasn't done
(2) Don't praise a person unless you can be sincere
(3) Don't be sparing in praise just because your superior withholds it from you
(4) Don't let too much time elapse between good performance and recognition of it

24. *HOW TO GAIN YOUR WORKERS' CONFIDENCE*
Methods of developing confidence include such things as:
(1) Knowing the interests, habits, hobbies of employees
(2) Admitting your own inadequacies
(3) Sharing and telling of confidence in others
(4) Supporting people when they are in trouble
(5) Delegating matters that can be well handled
(6) Being frank and straightforward about problems and working conditions
(7) Encouraging others to bring their problems to you
(8) Taking action on problems which impede worker progress

25. *SOURCES OF EMPLOYEE PROBLEMS*
On-the-job causes might be such things as:
(1) A feeling that favoritism is exercised in assignments
(2) Assignment of overtime
(3) An undue amount of supervision
(4) Changing methods or systems
(5) Stealing of ideas or trade secrets
(6) Lack of interest in job
(7) Threat of reduction in force
(8) Ignorance or lack of communications
(9) Poor equipment
(10) Lack of knowing how supervisor feels toward employee
(11) Shift assignments
Off-the-job problems might have to do with:
(1) Health (2) Finances (3) Housing (4) Family

26. *THE SUPERVISOR'S KEY TO DISCIPLINE*
There are several key points about discipline which the supervisor should keep in mind:
(1) Job discipline is one of the disciplines of life and is directed by the supervisor.
(2) It is more important to correct an employee fault than to fix blame for it.
(3) Employee performance is affected by problems both on the job and off.
(4) Sudden or abrupt changes in behavior can be indications of important employee problems.
(5) Problems should be dealt with as soon as possible after they are identified.
(6) The attitude of the supervisor may have more to do with solving problems than the techniques of problem solving.
(7) Correction of employee behavior should be resorted to only after the supervisor is sure that training or counseling will not be helpful
(8) Be sure to document your disciplinary actions.

(9) Make sure that you are disciplining on the basis of facts rather than personal feelings.

(10) Take each disciplinary step in order, being careful not to make snap judgments, or decisions based on impatience.

27. *FIVE IMPORTANT PROCESSES OF MANAGEMENT*

(1) Planning (2) Organizing (3) Scheduling
(4) Controlling (5) Motivating

28. *WHEN THE SUPERVISOR FAILS TO PLAN*

(1) Supervisor creates impression of not knowing his job
(2) May lead to excessive overtime
(3) Job runs itself-- supervisor lacks control
(4) Deadlines and appointments missed
(5) Parts of the work go undone
(6) Work interrupted by emergencies
(7) Sets a bad example
(8) Uneven workload creates peaks and valleys
(9) Too much time on minor details at expense of more important tasks

29. *FOURTEEN GENERAL PRINCIPLES OF MANAGEMENT*

(1) Division of work
(2) Authority and responsibility
(3) Discipline
(4) Unity of command
(5) Unity of direction
(6) Subordination of individual interest to general interest
(7) Remuneration of personnel
(8) Centralization
(9) Scalar chain
(10) Order
(11) Equity
(12) Stability of tenure of personnel
(13) Initiative
(14) Esprit de corps

30. *CHANGE*

Bringing about change is perhaps attempted more often, and yet less well understood, than anything else the supervisor does. How do people generally react to change? (People tend to resist change that is imposed upon them by other individuals or circumstances.)

Change is characteristic of every situation. It is a part of every real endeavor where the efforts of people are concerned.

A. Why do people resist change?

People may resist change because of:

(1) Fear of the unknown
(2) Implied criticism
(3) Unpleasant experiences in the past
(4) Fear of loss of status
(5) Threat to the ego
(6) Fear of loss of economic stability

B. How can we best overcome the resistance to change?

In initiating change, take these steps:

(1) Get ready to sell
(2) identify sources of help
(3) Anticipate objections
(4) Sell benefits
(5) Listen in depth
(6) Follow up

B. BRIEF TOPICAL SUMMARIES

I. WHO/WHAT IS THE SUPERVISOR?

1. The supervisor is often called the "highest level employee and the lowest level manager."
2. A supervisor is a member of both management and the work group. He acts as a bridge between the two.
3. Most problems in supervision are in the area of human relations, or people problems.
4. Employees expect: Respect, opportunity to learn and to advance, and a sense of belonging, and so forth.
5. Supervisors are responsible for directing people and organizing work. Planning is of paramount importance.
6. A position description is a set of duties and responsibilities inherent to a given position.
7. It is important to keep the position description up-to-date and to provide each employee with his own copy.

II. THE SOCIOLOGY OF WORK

1. People are alike in many ways; however each individual is unique.
2. The supervisor is challenged in getting to know employee differences. Acquiring skills in evaluating individuals is an asset.
3. Maintaining meaningful working relationships in the organization is of great importance.
4. The supervisor has an obligation to help individuals to develop to their fullest potential.
5. Job rotation on a planned basis helps to build versatility and to maintain interest and enthusiasm in work groups.
6. Cross training (job rotation) provides backup skills.
7. The supervisor can help reduce tension by maintaining a sense of humor, providing guidance to employees, and by making reasonable and timely decisions. Employees respond favorably to working under reasonably predictable circumstances.
8. Change is characteristic of all managerial behavior. The supervisor must adjust to changes in procedures, new methods, technological changes, and to a number of new and sometimes challenging situations.
9. To overcome the natural tendency for people to resist change, the supervisor should become more skillful in initiating change.

III. PRINCIPLES AND PRACTICES OF SUPERVISION

1. Employees should be required to answer to only one superior.
2. A supervisor can effectively direct only a limited number of employees,depending upon the complexity,variety,and proximity of the jobs involved.
3. The organizational chart presents the organization in graphic form. It reflects lines of authority and responsibility as well as interrelationships of units within the organization.
4. Distribution of work can be improved through an analysis using the "Work Distribution Chart."
5. The "Work Distribution Chart" reflects the division of work within a unit in understandable form.
6. When related tasks are given to an employee, he has a better chance of increasing his skills through training.
7. The individual who is given the responsibility for tasks must also be given the appropriate authority to insure adequate results.
8. The supervisor should delegate repetitive,routine work. Preparation of recurring reports,maintaining leave and attendance records are some examples.

9. Good discipline is essential to good task performance. Discipline is reflected in the actions of employees on the job in the absence of supervision.
10. Disciplinary action may have to be taken when the positive aspects of discipline have failed. Reprimand, warning, and suspension are examples of disciplinary action.
11. If a situation calls for a reprimand, be sure it is deserved and remember it is to be done in private.

IV. DYNAMIC LEADERSHIP

1. A style is a personal method or manner of exerting influence.
2. Authoritarian leaders often see themselves as the source of power and authority.
3. The democratic leader often perceives the group as the source of authority and power.
4. Supervisors tend to do better when using the pattern of leadership that is most natural for them.
5. Social scientists suggest that the effective supervisor use the leadership style that best fits the problem or circumstances involved.
6. All four styles -- telling, selling, consulting, joining -- have their place. Using one does not preclude using the other at another time.
7. The theory X point of view assumes that the average person dislikes work, will avoid it whenever possible, and must be coerced to achieve organizational objectives.
8. The theory Y point of view assumes that the average person considers work to be as natural as play, and, when the individual is committed, he requires little supervision or direction to accomplish desired objectives.
9. The leader's basic assumptions concerning human behavior and human nature affect his actions, decisions, and other managerial practices.
10. Dissatisfaction among employees is often present, but difficult to isolate. The supervisor should seek to weaken dissatisfaction by keeping promises, being sincere and considerate, keeping employees informed, and so forth.
11. Constructive suggestions should be encouraged during the natural progress of the work.

V. PROCESSES FOR SOLVING PROBLEMS

1. People find their daily tasks more meaningful and satisfying when they can improve them.
2. The causes of problems, or the key factors, are often hidden in the background. Ability to solve problems often involves the ability to isolate them from their backgrounds. There is some substance to the cliché that some persons "can't see the forest for the trees."
3. New procedures are often developed from old ones. Problems should be broken down into manageable parts. New ideas can be adapted from old ones.
4. People think differently in problem-solving situations. Using a logical, patterned approach is often useful. One approach found to be useful includes these steps:
   (a) Define the problem
   (b) Establish objectives
   (c) Get the facts
   (d) Weigh and decide
   (e) Take action
   (f) Evaluate action

VI. TRAINING FOR RESULTS

1. Participants respond best when they feel training is important to them.
2. The supervisor has responsibility for the training and development of those who report to him.
3. When training is delegated to others, great care must be exercised to insure the trainer has knowledge, aptitude, and interest for his work as a trainer.
4. Training (learning) of some type goes on continually. The most successful supervisor makes certain the learning contributes in a productive manner to operational goals.
5. New employees are particularly susceptible to training. Older employees facing new job situations require specific training, as well as having need for development and growth opportunities.
6. Training needs require continuous monitoring.
7. The training officer of an agency is a professional with a responsibility to assist supervisors in solving training problems.
8. Many of the self-development steps important to the supervisor's own growth are equally important to the development of peers and subordinates. Knowledge of these is important when the supervisor consults with others on development and growth opportunities.

VII. HEALTH,SAFETY, AND ACCIDENT PREVENTION

1. Management-minded supervisors take appropriate measures to assist employees in maintaining health and in assuring safe practices in the work environment.
2. Effective safety training and practices help to avoid injury and accidents.
3. Safety should be a management goal. All infractions of safety which are observed should be corrected without exception.
4. Employees'safety attitude, training and instruction, provision of safe tools and equipment, supervision, and leadership are considered highly important factors which contribute to safety and which can be influenced directly by supervisors.
5. When accidents do occur they should be investigated promptly for very important reasons, including the fact that information which is gained can be used to prevent accidents in the future.

VIII.EQUAL EMPLOYMENT OPPORTUNITY

1. The supervisor should endeavor to treat all employees fairly, without regard to religion, race, sex, or national origin.
2. Groups tend to reflect the attitude of the leader. Prejudice can be detected even in very subtle form. Supervisors must strive to create a feeling of mutual respect and confidence in every employee.
3. Complete utilization of all human resources is a national goal. Equitable consideration should be accorded women in the work force, minority-group members, the physically and mentally handicapped, and the older employee. The important question is: "Who can do the job?"
4. Training opportunities, recognition for performance, overtime assignments, promotional opportunities, and all other personnel actions are to be handled on an equitable basis.

IX. IMPROVING COMMUNICATIONS

1. Communications is achieving understanding between the sender and the receiver of a message. It also means sharing information -- the creation of understanding.
2. Communication is basic to all human activity. Words are means of conveying meanings; however, real meanings are in people.
3. There are very practical differences in the effectiveness of one-way, impersonal, and two-way communications. Words spoken face-to-face are better understood. Telephone conversations are effective, but lack the rapport of person-to-person exchanges. The whole person communicates.
4. Cooperation and communication in an organization go hand-in-hand. When there is a mutual respect between people, spelling out rules and procedures for communicating is unnecessary.
5. There are several barriers to effective communications. These include failure to listen with respect and understanding, lack of skill in feedback, and misinterpreting the meanings of words used by the speaker. It is also common practice to listen to what we want to hear, and tune out things we do not want to hear.
6. Communication is management's chief problem. The supervisor should accept the challenge to communicate more effectively and to improve interagency and intra-agency communications.
7. The supervisor may often plan for and conduct meetings. The planning phase is critical and may determine the success or the failure of a meeting.
8. Speaking before groups usually requires extra effort. Stage fright may never disappear completely, but it can be controlled.

X. SELF-DEVELOPMENT

1. Every employee is responsible for his own self-development.
2. Toastmaster and toastmistress clubs offer opportunities to improve skills in oral communications.
3. Planning for one's own self-development is of vital importance. Supervisors know their own strengths and limitations better than anyone else.
4. Many opportunities are open to aid the supervisor in his developmental efforts, including job assignments; training opportunities, both governmental and non-governmental -- to include universities and professional conferences and seminars.
5. Programmed instruction offers a means of studying at one's own rate.
6. Where difficulties may arise from a supervisor's being away from his work for training, he may participate in televised home study or correspondence courses to meet his self-development needs.

XI. TEACHING AND TRAINING

A. The Teaching Process

Teaching is encouraging and guiding the learning activities of students toward established goals. In most cases this process consists in five steps: preparation, presentation, summarization, evaluation, and application.

1. Preparation

Preparation is twofold in nature; that of the supervisor and the employee.

Preparation by the supervisor is absolutely essential to success. He must know what, when, where, how, and whom he will teach. Some of the factors that should be considered are:

(1) The objectives	(5) Employee interest
(2) The materials needed	(6) Training aids
(3) The methods to be used	(7) Evaluation
(4) Employee participation	(8) Summarization

Employee preparation consists in preparing the employee to receive the material. Probably the most important single factor in the preparation of the employee is arousing and maintaining his interest. He must know the objectives of the training, why he is there, how the material can be used, and its importance to him.

2. Presentation

In presentation, have a carefully designed plan and follow it. The plan should be accurate and complete, yet flexible enough to meet situations as they arise. The method of presentation will be determined by the particular situation and objectives.

3. Summary

A summary should be made at the end of every training unit and program. In addition, there may be internal summaries depending on the nature of the material being taught. The important thing is that the trainee must always be able to understand how each part of the new material relates to the whole.

4. Application

The supervisor must arrange work so the employee will be given a chance to apply new knowledge or skills while the material is still clear in his mind and interest is high. The trainee does not really know whether he has learned the material until he has been given a chance to apply it. If the material is not applied, it loses most of its value.

5. Evaluation

The purpose of all training is to promote learning. To determine whether the training has been a success or failure, the supervisor must evaluate this learning.

In the broadest sense evaluation includes all the devices, methods, skills, and techniques used by the supervisor to keep himself and the employees informed as to their progress toward the objectives they are pursuing. The extent to which the employee has mastered the knowledge, skills, and abilities, or changed his attitudes, as determined by the program objectives, is the extent to which instruction has succeeded or failed.

Evaluation should not be confined to the end of the lesson, day, or program but should be used continuously. We shall note later the way this relates to the rest of the teaching process.

B. Teaching Methods

A teaching method is a pattern of identifiable student and instructor activity used in presenting training material.

All supervisors are faced with the problem of deciding which method should be used at a given time.

1. Lecture

The lecture is direct oral presentation of material by the supervisor. The present trend is to place less emphasis on the trainer's activity and more on that of the trainee.

2. Discussion

Teaching by discussion or conference involves using questions and other techniques to arouse interest and focus attention upon certain areas, and by doing so creating a learning situation. This can be one of the most valuable methods because it gives the employees an opportunity to express their ideas and pool their knowledge.

3. Demonstration

The demonstration is used to teach how something works or how to do something. It can be used to show a principle or what the results of a series of actions will be. A well-staged demonstration is particularly effective because it shows proper methods of performance in a realistic manner.

4. Performance

Performance is one of the most fundamental of all learning techniques or teaching methods. The trainee may be able to tell how a specific operation should be performed but he cannot be sure he knows how to perform the operation until he has done so.

As with all methods, there are certain advantages and disadvantages to each method.

5. Which Method to Use

Moreover, there are other methods and techniques of teaching. It is difficult to use any method without other methods entering into it. In any learning situation a combination of methods is usually more effective than any one method alone.

Finally, evaluation must be integrated into the other aspects of the teaching-learning process.

It must be used in the motivation of the trainees; it must be used to assist in developing understanding during the training; and it must be related to employee application of the results of training.

This is distinctly the role of the supervisor.

BASIC FUNDAMENTALS of

EVIDENCE

CONTENTS

BASIC FUNDAMENTALS
of
EVIDENCE

COMMENTARY

The following section presents a concisely abridged, generalized outline of the rules of evidence and procedures based upon rules developed and enunciated in laws, court decisions, and corollary sources.

I. PURPOSES

Paraphrasing a court decision, the purpose of evidence is to inform the trier of the case of the competent, relevant and material facts bearing upon the issues, in order that the truth may be elicited and a just determination of the controversy reached.

The following points characterize the rules of evidence:

1. They have been tested by years of experience and have been found effective to do justice.
2. They have evolved and changed gradually, in keeping with the times and the development of the law. They have been adapted to meet new situations created by the onward march of technology and science.
3. They are important to know as to what is or is not admissible, in order to "gather in" the reliable evidence.
4. Their purpose is to establish the truth.
5. They confine trials to the germane issues of the controversy.
6. They are designed to reduce delays during trials, by excluding excursions into matters foreign to and outside the germane issues.
7. They are comparable to the "rules of the game" in contested sports.

8. They are brought into play while the "contest" is on.
9. They are used in evaluating the entire record, in order to arrive at a correct and just decision.
10. They are the necessary tools to enable a judge to do justice to all.

II. DEFINITIONS

Evidence is the legal term which covers all of the information and facts adduced in a case, be it testimony of witnesses, or documents or other objects identified by witnesses, or otherwise admissible and presented to the court to prove or disprove the facts in issue.

Evidence is the medium of proof.

Proof is the effect or result of evidence in convincing the mind of the trier of the facts. It is the conclusion arrived at by a consideration of the evidence.

Testimony is the oral part of evidence consisting of the statements of witnesses made under oath.

Facts and Circumstances

A *fact* is what a witness has seen, heard, smelled, felt or tasted (the five senses). The general rule is that a witness must speak of facts alone. He may not utter opinions, conclusions or inferences. (See later discussion on Opinion for certain exceptions).

Circumstances are collections of facts.

Inferences may be drawn from facts and circumstances. Inferences are reasonable deductions or conclusions flowing logically from facts which have been proved.

Conclusions are statements a witness makes and believes but did not himself witness or know of his own knowledge. They may be based on two or more separate facts.

Kinds of Evidence

Direct evidence is proof of the facts in issue, communicated to the trier of the facts by witnesses, having actual knowledge of them by means of their senses. It is that evidence which, without inference or evidence of any other facts, tends to establish directly a fact in issue.

Circumstantial Evidence is proof of collateral facts, where circumstances are shown, from which the inference may be drawn that the principal or essential facts are true and existed, in such a way that the proof is irreconcilable with any other theory that can be presented.

Circumstantial evidence may be good evidence and should not be ignored.

Documentary evidence consists of writings, instruments, inscriptions and documents of all kinds.

Real Evidence is evidence of which the trier of the facts acquires knowledge by personal observation and inspection of a thing or object to which the testimony refers. It may be a physical object, inspection of premises or exhibition of parts of the body.

NOTE: If real evidence is received, it should be minutely described on the record.

Pictures—photographs, snapshots, moving pictures which are true and authenticated representations, also x-ray plates, (which are authenticated by a professional witness) are admissible.

Diagrams and Models which are explained by a witness knowing how they were made and what they represent.

NOTE: Diagrams may be made in the course of a hearing by a witness, who is qualified to make them. They are subject to cross-examination, if they are challenged as to reliability or relevancy.

Maps, either official, or made by a witness before or during a hearing. In the latter event, they are subject to cross-examination, if they are challenged as to reliability or relevancy.

Positive Evidence—Proof that a certain fact does exist or did exist.

Negative Evidence—Proof that a certain fact does not exist or did not ever exist. Usually, positive evidence as to a particular fact is considered stronger in weight than negative evidence as to the same fact.

"Prima Facie" Evidence (The Latin phrase, *prima facie* literally means "at first view").—*Prima facie* evidence is evidence, which if unexplained or uncontradicted, establishes a fact alleged, or raises a presumption of fact.

Self Serving Evidence or Testimony—Testimony, statements, or documents submitted as evidence which are self-serving or in a person's own favor are usually inadmissible in evidence in a court of law because of the danger that they were fabricated to aid his case.

NOTE: However, they may be received for what they are worth in an administrative hearing and weighed in the evaluation of substantial evidence.

Telephone Conversations—Before proof of telephone conversations may be admitted, it is necessary that the identity of the speaker be sufficiently authenticated.

Such authentication may be based on recognition of the voice based on prior or subsequent conversations with the same person or may be based on the actions of the speaker subsequent to the telephone conversation.

III. STIPULATIONS

Parties may make stipulations between themselves which may even stipulate away their statutory or constitutional rights, which are exclusively matters of private right and no consideration of public policy or morals is involved.

Parties may stipulate to offer evidence which is not strictly evidence to establish a material fact.

Where parties enter into a stipulation with regard to the facts in a case for the purpose of evidence, it is in the case until the litigation is ended or until the trier of the case, upon application, relieves the party therefrom. Such relief may be granted in instances of fraud or mistake.

However, parties cannot stipulate what the law is.

IV. FACTS AND OPINIONS

Facts are given by witnesses having personal knowledge (see definition of Facts, *supra*).

Opinions may be given by lay persons or by experts. They are reasoning based on facts.

By Lay Persons

A lay person may give his opinion based upon common ordinary knowledge, without special skill or background. His opinion may pertain to the following subjects, for example:

Observations—A lay person may give his opinion as to such matters as color, weight, distance, size, quantity, state of emotion, apparent physical condition, identity and likeness, estimated age, rational or irrational conduct, handwriting.

Sensations—A lay person may describe his own sensory experiences, such as taste, smell and touch. He may testify as to heat or cold or electric shock.

Emotions—A lay person may give his opinion of another person's display of emotion. He may state, for example, that one person's contact with another was friendly or hostile.

Intention—Where the actual performance of an act is not disputed, but its effect or genuineness depends upon the intent with which it was done, the one who did it may testify as to what his intention was at the time.

Physical or Mental Condition—A lay person may describe another person's apparent physical condition, such as general strength, vigor, feebleness, illness or any other characteristics that anyone can see; or whether a person appeared to be intoxicated. The necessary foundation for an expression of opinion as to apparent intoxication of another may include testimony that the person in question smelled of alcohol, was incoherent in speech, his eyes were glassy or bloodshot, he could not stand or walk without assistance, etc. He may also testify as to rational or irrational conduct of a person.

Identification of Voice—As to evidence of telephone conversations see Telephone conversations, *supra*. The same standards control testimony as to the identification of a voice of a person who is heard but is out of sight.

Speed—A lay person may testify that a vehicle was moving rapidly or slowly. However, if he testifies as to the rate of speed, he must first show that he has had some experience in observing the rate of travel of vehicles or give some other satisfactory reason or basis for his opinion.

Age—A lay person may give his estimate of another person's apparent age. However, the facts and circumstances upon which his opinion is based must be given and the witness should first describe the person's appearance and only then give his own opinion as to his age.

One may testify as to his own age.

Value—See Evidence of Value *infra.*

Handwriting—See Handwriting *infra.*

Identification—The identification by a lay person of someone whom he knows or has seen before is proper, even though it may not be positive and absolutely certain. Although it need not be beyond any doubt, it must, nevertheless, be based upon some convincing and reliable sensory impression, the description of which raises the likelihood that it is the same person. Identification of automobiles may be based upon customary experience and from the observation of cars which would qualify a lay person to testify with some knowledge on this subject.

By Experts

Opinion evidence by an expert witness is admissible to meet the necessity of providing to the trier of the facts, the aid of those especially qualified by education, background, experience, training and study to express an opinion on questions of fact relating to particular skills, art, science, business, technology, medicine and other matters requiring special knowledge.

Experts must be qualified by preliminary examination as to their particular education, background and knowledge on the specific subject. They cannot testify as to matters of common knowledge. The question, as to whether there is need for expert testimony is in the trial judge's discretion.

An expert may not be compelled to give his opinion against his will unless he can give testimony based on direct observation or experience.

There are two general types of expert testimony; knowledge as to facts and knowledge giving rise to conclusions to be drawn from facts.

Unless the judge orders otherwise, questions calling for the opinion of an expert witness need not be hypothetical.

The subjects calling for expert testimony may be in the fields of science, engineering, medicine, handwriting, or intoxicated driving tests or in any other areas of knowledge, requiring special study, training, experience or other qualifications. Opinion evidence may be called for to support facts as to cause and effect, values, cause of injury or death, mental condition or damages.

V. AFFIDAVIT

An affidavit is a statement sworn to before a person authorized to take oaths and acknowledgements.

VI. DEPOSITION

A sworn statement of a witness, usually taken pursuant to judicial order or consent of the parties, in the taking of which both sides are or have an opportunity to be present so that the opposing party may cross-examine the witness.

VII. RELEVANCY OF EVIDENCE

The dictionary definition of "relevant" is "related to the matter at hand, to the point, pertinent."

In law, what is relevant relates in some logical way to the principal fact. Relevant evidence is evidence which is germane to the issues in dispute. Broadly, it is that which bears directly, as distinguished from collaterally, upon the point or facts in issue, and which tends to prove or disprove the matters in issue.

A fact is relevant to another fact when, according to the common course of events, the existence of one, either by itself or in connection with other facts, proves or renders probable, the existence of the other.

Irrelevant evidence is evidence which does not affect the disputed issues of fact. As Gilbert and Sullivan phrased it, "the flowers that bloom in the spring, tra, la, have nothing to do with the case." They are irrelevant.

Generally, evidence is irrelevant, if the purpose of showing that a person did a particular thing at one time is to prove that he did a similar thing at another time.

Exceptions are where such proof is intended to show a regular or continuous course of conduct or to prove notice of certain facts.

Generally, the fact that a person is an habitual litigant is irrelevant. So too, acts of other persons under the same circumstances are irrelevant. Generally, the wealth or poverty of a person is irrelevant.

Proof of prior dealings between the same parties may be relevant to show authority to act or agency.

Material evidence is that which is relevant to the case.

VIII. COMPETENT EVIDENCE

NOTE: This subject is further developed in treating with the competency of witnesses to testify under Competency of Witnesses and Privileged Relationships, *infra*.

The dictionary definition of "competent" as applied to law is: "legally qualified or fit; admissible".

Competent evidence is relevant evidence which is not barred by an exclusionary rule.

Incompetent evidence may relate to unsworn testimony, interest or privilege.

IX. JUDICIAL NOTICE

NOTE: In administrative adjudication, this principle is also called "official notice". What follows may be adapted by hearing officers in keeping with the exigencies of the case.

Judicial notice is the notice which a judge will officially take of a fact without receiving evidence with respect thereto. It takes the place of proof. It dispenses with the necessity of offering evidence as to notorious facts, which are generally known. It is exercised only by the trier of the facts.

Judicial notice may be taken by a judge, on his own motion or at the request of a party. Judicial notice may be taken (1) of such facts which are so generally known or of such common notoriety that they cannot reasonably be the subject of dispute or (2) specific facts and propositions of generalized knowledge which are capable of immediate and accurate determination by resort to easily accessible sources of indisputable accuracy or (3) generally recognized technical or scientific facts within the judge's knowledge.

However, parties should be notified of any facts as to which judicial notice is taken, and be afforded an opportunity to contest the correctness of the facts so noticed.

The principle of judicial notice is most flexible and elastic. New applications are made with the constantly changing conditions of society and the continuing diversity of facts presented to the courts.

Examples:

Matters of Fact

- Historical events
- The course and laws of nature
- Mortality tables
- Intoxicating nature of beverages
- Geographical facts
- Census statistics
- Meteorological data on a certain day
- Official weather reports
- Existence of departments and poltical subdivisions of government
- Public officers, past and present
- Jurisdiction, powers and records of the court in which the judge sits
- Meaning of words, phrases and abbreviations

Matters of Law

- Statutes of the State
- Acts of Congress
- Legislature of the State
- Traffic regulations
- Court procedures
- Authority of public officers
- Laws of other states
- Laws of foreign countries, if a party requests it and furnishes the court with sufficient information to enable it to comply with the request.

X. PRESUMPTIONS

A presumption is an inference drawn from particular facts or particular evidence, unless and until the truth of the inference is disproved. A presumption may be indulged in to supply the place of facts. However, a presumption disappears in the presence of substantial evidence to the contrary.

There are two kinds of presumptions; presumptions of fact and presumptions of law.

Of Fact

A presumption of fact is made upon principles of induction. It is an inference drawn by a logical process of reasoning from observation, experience or other admitted facts.

Every inference must stand upon some clear, direct evidence and not upon some other inference or presumption.

Of Law

Presumptions may be part of the law itself; for example, Section 21 of the Workmen's Compensation Law.

There are two kinds of presumptions of law; a conclusive one and a rebuttable one.

A conclusive presumption of law forbids inquiry into the real facts. It becomes a rule of substantive law.

Examples:

Everyone is presumed to know the law.

A sane person, acting voluntarily, knowingly and wilfully, intends that which is the natural and necessary consequence of his acts.

A written contract is presumed to incorporate the entire agreement between the parties thereto (subject to actions in equity to relieve a party from that presumption). See discussion under Parol Evidence Rule *infra.*

The statute of limitations bars a debt after six years, unless it is kept alive in certain ways.

A release in writing is binding without consideration, provided it is signed by the party against whom one seeks to enforce it.

A rebuttable presumption of law may be overcome by proper evidence. It is subject to the same condition as a presumption of fact, in that it disappears when substantial evidence to the contrary is introduced.

Examples:

It is presumed that a public official, a fiduciary, an officer or director of a corporation will not do anything contrary to his official duty or fail to do anything which his official duty requires him to do.

Legislative enactments are presumed to be constitutional, subject to legal action to prove otherwise.

NOTE: An administrative tribunal has no power to rule upon constitutionality of any law. That power is reserved to the courts. However, an administrative tribunal may rule upon the question of whether or not an official has exercised his powers unconstitutionally.

It is presumed that a marriage ceremony was properly and legally performed. The validity of a marriage is presumed.

Every child is presumed legitimate, even in the absence of proof that he was born in wedlock.

The intentional suppression, destruction or fabrication of relevant evidence raises the presumption that the truth would have militated against the responsible party.

Withholding or failing to produce evidence, which is available to a party and which he ordinarily would be expected to produce, raises a presumption that the evidence was held back because it was unfavorable.

Failure to call an available witness, who is likely to be favorable, raises an unfavorable presumption.

Everyone is presumed to be sane until the contrary is shown. Insanity is not presumed from an act of suicide. The presumption is in favor of mistake, or accident, rather than suicide.

Identity of name presumes the identity of person, especially where there is a similarity of residence or occupation or other coincidental circumstances or where the name is unusual.

It is presumed that an instrument or document was made on its date and that it was delivered at the time of its date. Delivery is presumed from possession thereof.

Solvency is presumed until the contrary is shown.

It is presumed that a person in possession of personal property is its owner.

The continuance of life is presumed.

The continuance of domicile, citizenship, partnership is presumed.

Other Examples of General Presumptions

A fact continuous in its nature is presumed to continue to exist.

The continuance of a law in force is presumed.

Innocence is presumed in a criminal proceeding. It does not apply in a civil action because there, the rule of preponderance of evidence applies.

Knowledge of the contents of their books is presumed when members of a firm have access to them and an opportunity to know how their accounts were kept.

Mailing of letters: It is presumed that a properly addressed and stamped envelope, deposited in a post office or regularly maintained post box, reaches it destination. If the proof is that such mailing was in a course of business or office practice, it raises the presumption that it was in fact mailed. However, there must be a foundation laid showing that the letter was placed in the usual office receptacle for outgoing mail and the person whose duty it is to mail such letters testifies that he always mails such letters placed in such receptacle, and what procedure he follows.

Telegrams are presumed to be delivered, if properly addressed and transmitted.

It is presumed that public officers do their duty in good faith.

Proof of the ownership of a motor vehicle createes a presumption that the person operating it, did so with the owner's permission.

Where alleged services are rendered by a relative or close friend, it is presumed, in the absence of agreement, that they were rendered voluntarily, gratuitously and without expectation of pay therefor.

Where there are conflicting presumptions of unequal weight, the stronger will prevail.

No Presumptions

Fraudulent intent is not presumed.

Payment is not presumed by lapse of time, except where various Statutes of Limitations which outlaw certain debts and obligations apply.

XI. ADMISSIONS

An admission is a statement or act which amounts to the affirmance of some material fact, where such affirmance operates against the interest of the person making it or doing it.

An admission must be factual. It must be an acknowledgement of a relevant fact or the adoption of a statement made by another person in regard thereto. It may not be the expression of an opinion or intention or as to matters of law.

An admission against interest is any statement made by a person, or attributable to him, which tends to establish or disprove any material fact in the case against him.

Admissions by a person of any fact material to the issue are always competent evidence against him, whenever, wherever or to whomever made.

An admission may be explained away by either a person's own testimony or by introducing other evidence designed to explain the apparent inconsistency between the alleged admission and the present claim.

An admission made through mistake may be rejected.

An admission of a person may be admissible even though not based on personal knowledge.

An admission may be by conduct which is inconsistent with a person's position in the case being tried.

An admission may be by silence when the person hears and fully comprehends the force and effect of the words spoken and when he is at full liberty to reply thereto and would naturally be expected to deny it, if he considered it false. No presumption of acquiesence would arise, if the person, at the time of the statement was asleep, intoxicated, deaf, unable to fully understand the language used, or incapacitated or in any way deprived of the freedom or opportunity to reply.

Acts and declarations of an agent within the scope of his authority and part of the *res gestae* (see definition *infra*) are admissible against the principal, whether at the time the evidence is offered, the agent is living or dead.

Declarations of an officer of a corporation in a matter affecting the business of the corporation and in respect to which he was acting for it, are admissible as evidence against the corporation.

A member of a partnership is the general agent of the firm in relation to all of the business of the firm and can bind the partnership in what he says and does in such business.

Admissions or declarations by a person who is a joint owner may be taken against himself and the other party having a joint interest.

Proof of an admission made in former testimony may be given by anyone who heard it without producing the minutes of the former proceeding.

An admission by a person may be deduced, if a prior statement was made by him, which is contrary to the position he later takes in the case.

There are judicial and extra-judicial admissions. Judicial admissions may be formal or informal. Examples of a formal judicial admission are admitting the genuineness of a paper or photograph; admission under an agreed state of facts or a stipulation (unless relieved therefrom by the court); facts admitted by the pleadings (complaint, answer, reply). An informal judicial admission may be facts incidentally admitted in the course of a trial in the same or another case; facts admitted in a deposition or affidavit.

Extra-judicial admissions are the admissions of a person or his legal representative, which are oral, written or by conduct, which are not made in the course of the case on trial. They are admissible to show a position which is inconsistent with the person's present claim with respect to relevant facts in issue. They are then deemed admissions against interest discussed above.

XII. HEARSAY

Hearsay is evidence which, whether orally or in writing, seeks to establish the existence of a fact based not upon the witness' own personal knowledge or observation but on what someone else said.

A common example is; C testifies as to what B said about A who is a party to the proceeding. B is not present to testify.

Hearsay may be a rumor as to what a person said or did. An example is when a witness testifies that the "pipeline" in an office was to the effect that a person was neglecting his duties regularly.

Hearsay may be gossip in a place of employment such as; that a person was living beyond his means.

Hearsay is second-hand evidence and may be utterly untrustworthy. The basic objection to it is that it infringes on the right of confrontation and cross-examination and may hurt the person against whom it is directed, without giving him the protection of these constitutional rights.

In a court of law, hearsay is generally inadmissible over the objection of an opposing party. However, hearsay is admissible in an administrative hearing, for what it is worth. It may give the hearing officer leads upon which he may base his examination of witnesses. It may afford the hearing officer the opportunity to bring in by notice or subpoena, the alleged author of the hearsay statement, oral or written, if the subject matter thereof is crucial to a fair disposition of the issues.

The mere admission of hearsay evidence in an administrative hearing in not by itself sufficient to invalidate a decision therein, if in the record there is other reliable, probative and substantial evidence.

Other Examples of Hearsay

Reports of administrative agencies
Reports of mercantile agencies
Experts' reports
Prior declarations of deceased persons
Statistical tables

Exceptions to Hearsay

There are exceptions to the rule against hearsay, even in courts of law, based on necessity or due to the difficulty of obtaining direct proof, or the circumstantial guarantee of trustworthiness arising from the circumstances under which the statements were made.

Some of these are entries, notes or memoranda made in the regular course of business (see Business Records and Shop Book Rule, *infra*).

Dying Declarations are not received in civil actions unless part of the *res gestae* (see next paragraph).

XIII. "RES GESTAE" RULE

The Latin phrase *res gestae* means literally "things done." Under this rule, evidence of certain acts, statements, facts and circumstances which are so closely related to the question in issue as to be considered part of the "things done" and which are not normally admissible under other rules of evidence (such as hearsay) is admissible. *Res gestae* statements may tend to elucidate and explain the character and quality of the act which they accompany.

Examples

Spontaneous statements made under the influence of a startling event, occasion or condition and made on the spur of the moment and before the speaker has had time for mental reflection are received as part of the *res gestae,* regardless of the speaker's interests or implication in the main event. If a person involved in an automobile accident says on contact with the other object or immediately thereafter, "my brakes did not work," this is a classic example of *res gestae* and may be used in testimony against him.

If an agent makes authorized statements and admissions concerning his acts, provided the statements and admissions are made at the same time, the principal will be bound under the *res gestae* rule.

Involuntary expressions of pain are admissible under this rule.

XIV. BUSINESS RECORDS AND SHOP BOOK RULE

Any writing or record, entry, memorandum of any act, transaction, occurrence or event is admissible in evidence in proof of said act, occurrence or event, if it was made in the regular course of any business, profession, occupation or calling of any kind and it was the regular course of such business, etc., to make such memorandum or record at the same time of such act, transaction, occurrence or event, or within a reasonable time thereafter. This is known familiarly as the Shop Book Rule.

It is emphasized that this exception to the hearsay rule embraces only those entries which are made systematically in the regular routine and usual course of the business, etc. It does not embrace entries made as isolated transactions or incidents or for a specific purpose which is the subject of the litigation or hearing.

NOTE: This shop book rule comes into play frequently in administrative hearings. Official records, showing the history of a case, probably made by several different persons, in the discharge of their duties, are clearly admissible under this rule.

Examples

Books of account

Written memoranda of public officers

Police blotters (excluding hearsay matters)

Hospital records, covering
- diagnosis,
- prognosis,
- treatment,
- certified bills,

(but do not include hearsay statements of how injuries were sustained or illness contracted unless admissible under another exception to the hearsay rule).

XV. PUBLIC RECORDS AND DOCUMENTS

Books, documents, and records of a public nature required by law to be kept are *prima facie* evidence because they are made by disinterested persons in the discharge of public duties, with no reason to falsify such entries.

Particular Records

Birth Certificate is evidence of birth but not as proof of facts recited therein.

Marriage Certificate is evidence of marriage but not as proof of facts recited therein.

Death Certificate is only evidence of fact of death but not as to the cause of death or other data therein.

Maps. Certain maps are presumptive evidence of the matters of fact stated therein.

Weather Reports by the official Weather Bureau are *prima facie* evidence of the matters of fact stated therein.

Copies of Public Records

Certified or authenticated copies of papers filed in a public office may be received in evidence.

Official transcripts of public records, certified or authenticated, are also admissible.

Records from Other Jurisdictions

Laws, records, judicial proceedings of any state or court thereof, if properly attested and certified are admissible in evidence, under the full faith and credit clause of the United States Constitution.

Federal records, properly attested and certified are also admissible.

Jurisdictional Facts in Court Records

It is presumed that a court of general common law or constitutional jurisdiction, acted in accordance with the rules of practice governing it and did not act until every prerequisite prescribed by law was complied with; that its power was properly invoked and its process duly served and that its judgment, in form, is at least *prima facie* evidence of a legal judgment.

XVI. BEST EVIDENCE RULE

NOTE: This rule is a good example of an inclusionary rule which should guide a hearing officer in obtaining the best evidence available. This is a classic illustration of the soundness of established rules of evidence.

This rule requires a party to produce the best evidence of which the case in its nature is susceptible. The best evidence should be obtained because it is reliable. The best evidence is original or primary evidence, as distinguished from secondary evidence. It should include the best evidence which is procurable in the circumstances.

For example, the best evidence of what a person did is that of an eye witness; the best evidence of what an object looks like is the object itself; a written instrument is itself the primary or best evidence of its existence and contents. A copy or the recollection of a witness, is secondary evidence.

The principle of this rule is intended to prevent fraud, fabrication, or mistake and to eliminate uncertainties that may result from faulty memories.

Secondary Evidence

Upon objection thereto, the use of substitute or secondary evidence is barred when the original or primary evidence can be obtained. Before secondary evidence can be received properly, a valid legal reason must be given to account for the fact that the original cannot be produced. A proper foundation must be laid for the receipt of secondary evidence, such as showing that the original writing has been destroyed or lost; or that it is unobtainable because it is out of the jurisdiction; or that it is in the adverse party's possession or control and he has refused to produce it. Secondary evidence of the contents of a writing may not be given until its absence is satisfactorily explained.

Generally

Trustworthy copies such as photostats may be admissible in the first instance.

If a writing is collateral to the principal fact, it is not necessary to produce it. Collateral matters are not within the rule.

The invoking of the best evidence rule is illustrated in the simple instance of a letter. While a carbon copy may ordinarily be accepted, upon laying a foundation therefor, if the original letter is obtainable, it may present other facets of evidence. The signature thereon may be questioned as to whether it was authorized or authentic. The original letter may have a handwritten postscript or other writing placed upon the letter before it was mailed and which will not show on a carbon copy.

XVII. PAROL EVIDENCE RULE

"Parol" in law means "an utterance given by word of mouth."

When an agreement is reduced to writing, it is deemed, as between the parties thereto, to merge into it and supersede all prior negotiations and deliberation on the subject matter thereof, between the parties.

The parol evidence rule bars any oral testimony to vary, contradict, explain, add to or subtract from its terms, except as noted below. This rule protects against fraud, fabrication, perjury, the failure of memory or disadvantages resulting from deaths of witnesses.

The parol evidence rule applies only to the parties to the writing. It may not be invoked for or against a stranger to the writing.

Exceptions

Matters may be proved to show invalidity, fraud, duress, mistake, illegality, lack of consideration, lack of capacity to contract, material alteration or any other matter affecting the binding effect of the writing.

If the writing is incomplete on its face or does not contain the entire agreement, parol evidence, not inconsistent with its terms, may be received, not to contradict the writing but to show the real and true contract.

If the writing is ambiguous and not clear, oral testimony is admissible only for the purpose of explaining the particular ambiguity.

Parol evidence may be offered to show that a writing was delivered conditionally or in escrow.

Parol evidence may be offered to show an oral agreement which was independent of or collateral to the writing, provided it does not contradict the express or implied provisions of the writing.

Subsequent parol modifications of a writing may be proven to show a new and distinct agreement upon a new consideration, whether it be a substitute for the original writing or in addition to and beyond it. If the oral modification has been acted upon by one of the parties, to his disavantage in reliance upon such modification, it may be shown to establish a waiver or estoppel against the party who induced the other to change his position to his disadvantage.

Parol evidence concerning a writing may be offered to prove; the true consideration therefor; the true date of its execution; the purpose of its execution; the meaning of technical terms; the meaning of words or terms which usage has given therein in a particular trade or business or in a particular locality.

XVIII. THE STATUTE OF FRAUDS

Its purpose is to prevent frauds.

To satisfy the Statute of Frauds, a writing must contain all the material terms of an agreement signed by the party to be charged or his duly authorized agent; otherwise, the exceptions to the Parol Evidence rule (discussed *supra*) may apply.

The Statute provides mainly; that certain contracts must be in writing. These are:

- Contracts not to be performed within one year.
- Contracts to answer for the debt, default or miscarriage of another.
- Contracts to sell or for the sale of goods of the value of over $500, unless the goods are accepted in part, or earnest money is given, or part payment is made where the contract is signed by the party or his agent.
- Contracts to sell an interest in realty, other than a lease for a term not exceeding one year.

Exceptions

After its execution, a written contract may be modified by a subsequent contract, written or oral.

The extension of time for the performance of a contract may be oral. That the original contract has been modified may be proved by circumstantial evidence, by showing the conduct of the parties.

XIX. EVIDENCE OF VALUE

Opinions of witnesses may be received on questions of value of real or personal property or services, subject to qualification and cross-examination.

Opinions as to value may be given by experts who are qualified to speak on the subject. (See Facts and Opinions, *supra,* as to the qualifications of expert witnesses). Even though a witness is not qualified as an expert in the field, he may testify as to value, where it is shown that he has somewhat more knowledge of the particular facts in issue, than the trier of the facts.

Opinions may be given of the value of real estate, a plant, a stock of goods of any tangible property, or of the goodwill of business.

An owner of an automobile is qualified to testify as to its value.

A person is qualified to testify as to the value of his own servies.

XX. HANDWRITING

Comparison of a disputed writing, including a signature, with any writing proved satisfactorily to be the genuine handwriting or signature of any person is permitted. The witness need not be an expert. His comparison may be made on the basis of his acquaintance and familiarity with the hand-writing of the person involved.

Opinions of a handwriting expert may be based upon his comparison of the disputed writing with any writing proved to be the handwriting of the person alleged to have made the disputed handwriting. He usually testifies as to the writer's habits in the formation of letters, words, spacing, alignment, abbreviations, etc. He can then give his opinion as to whether the disputed and proven writings were made by the same hand.

Opinions of a handwriting expert must be tested in a most thorough manner by cross-examination. His competence as an expert may be contradicted or challenged by the testimony of other witnesses.

The same conditions apply to handprinting.

Typewriting

Expert testimony may be received to prove that two typewritten papers were typed on the same machine. The same conditions as to qualifications and cross-examination apply here too.

XXI. CORPORATIONS

The acts of corporations may be proved in the same way as the acts of individuals. The corporation acts only through individuals.

It is not necessary to prove the adoption of a formal resolution at a corporate meeting in order to give evidence of any action taken.

With regard to small corporations, it is not necessary to show that action was taken pursuant to a formal vote.

Corporate books are competent evidence of corporate acts.

A corporation may be bound by acts of duly authorized employees or agents in the same way that a natural person may be bound and it is not necessary to prove the adoption of a formal resolution with regard thereto.

The president of a corporation, who is its executive officer has power, *prima facie,* to do any act which the directors can authorize or ratify.

XXII. BURDEN OF PROOF

NOTE: What follows is an outline of the rules of practice and procedure established by the courts in civil cases. Such rules arise from the obligations imposed upon parties, as disclosed by the claims and the defenses or counterclaims made by parties to a law suit, as set forth in their pleadings. This subject is discussed herein as part of the law of evidence.

The burden of proof is defined as the obligation imposed upon a plaintiff in making his claim and upon a defendant in asserting affirmative defenses and counterclaims, to persuade the trier of the facts by a fair preponderance of the evidence, of the truth of what each has affirmatively asserted in his pleadings. Although the duty of going forward with the evidence (for instance, when a defendand satisfactorily meets the *prima facie* case of a plaintiff and the plaintiff must submit more proof to overcome the defense of the defendant), may shift several times during the course of a trial, the burden of proof never shifts. If at the end of a trial, the evidence is evenly balanced, the verdict must be against the party who has the burden of proof, because he has failed to prove his case by a fair preponderance of the evidence.

The burden of proof rests upon public agencies, as well as on private parties who have the affirmative on any issue. Proof must be based on evidence, not conjecture. *Prima facie* evidence of a cause of action is sufficient to sustain the burden of proof until met and disputed by competent affirmative evidence offered by the other party.

Preponderance of Evidence

This means the greater weight of the evidence. In a civil case, the plaintiff must establish his claim by a fair preponderance of the evidence. Likewise, the defendant must establish his affirmative defenses and his counterclaims by the same standard.

In weighing the evidence, there may be taken into consideration the attitude, appearances and acts of the parties and witnesses and there may be deduced therefrom such inferences as may fairly arise out of the given circumstances.

The advantage of the trier of the case who saw and heard the witnesses and observed their demeanor on the witness stand should be considered on appeal or review. When the truth depends upon the credibility of witnesses, the conclusions of the trier of the case based on credibility should be given the greatest weight.

Failure to Produce Evidence Within Control

Where a party, knowing the truth of a matter in controversy, and having the necessary evidence in his possession, omits to speak, every inference warranted by the evidence offered will be indulged against him because of his failure to speak.

Unfavorable inferences, as warranted by the evidence, may be drawn against a party when he fails to call a material witness under his control; but such inferences do not amount to an admission of the truth of the evidence of the other party. A *prima facie* case, at least, must still be made out by the party having the burden of proof. If the failure to testify or furnish evidence is satisfactorily explained, no unfavorable inference may be drawn therefrom.

Fraud

The burden of proving fraud is upon the party asserting it and, as with other facts must be established by a fair preponderance of the evidence.

Fraud must be proved and not presumed. Suspicion is not enough.

Where evidence is equally as consistent with innocence as with wrongdoing, the innocent construction should be adopted.

Gifts

No presumption is created in the law in favor of gifts. Proof of intent and delivery is required.

"Res Ipsa Loquitur"

This Latin phrase means "the thing speaks for itself." This rule is commonly applied in an accident case where the thing which caused an injury was exclusively under the defendant's control and an accident is proven which ordinarily could not have happened without negligence. Then the mere occurrence of the accident may be sufficient to raise the inference of negligence on the part of the defendant.

The rule is also applied where the circumstances involved or connected with an accident are of such unusual character as to justify, in the absence of other evidence bearing on the matter, the inference that the accident was due to the negligence of the one having possession or control of the thing causing the injury.

A common example is where a person is walking on a public sidewalk and he is struck by an object falling from some place in the building, in front of which he was passing. The circumstances of such accident furnish some *prima facie* evidence. However, this does not relieve the plaintiff from the burden of proof. It stays with him and does not shift to the defendant. He still must prove his case by a fair preponderance of the evidence.

"Prima Facie" Case

When the party who has the burden of proof has produced sufficient evidence to be entitled to a judgment in his favor, a *prima facie* case has been made out. When the other side presents his evidence, he may overcome the *prima facie* case. This calls for going forward with the evidence in rebuttal.

"Res Judicata"

This Latin phrase means "the thing adjudicated". An existing final judgment rendered upon the merits by a court of competent jurisdiction is conclusive of the rights of the parties or their privies in any and all other actions between the same parties on the controverted points of issue which were adjudicated in the first suit.

NOTE: This situation arises occasionally in administrative hearings. Where there has been a decision in a controversy between an agency and another party and either party requests a hearing on the identical issues (sometimes in substitution for an appeal or review), the hearing officer may dismiss the second proceeding under the doctrine of *res judicata,* provided of course, the parties and the issues and the periods involved are identical.

XXIII. COMPETENCY OF WITNESSES

Judges (Hearing Officers)

The testimony of a judge or a hearing officer in a case in which he sits as a judge or hearing officer is incompetent. He cannot assume two roles which conflict with each other; first as a witness, then as an adjudicator who passes upon the worth of his own testimony. No man can be a judge of his own cause.

The competency rule is commonly applied in dealing with the mental capacity of a person to testify.

As we have seen under Competent Evidence, *supra,* "competent" as applied to law is defined as "legally qualified or fit; admissible."

Adults and Teen-Agers

If objection is made that a witness is incompetent mentally, the trier of the case must inquire fully and completely into the mental capacity of the witness to testify.

Children

If the competency of a child of tender years is in doubt, the trier of the case must inquire fully and completely into his capacity to testify and the extent of his knowledge and intelligence.

The Value of an Oath

In both of the above instances, inquiry must be made as to whether or not the witness can comprehend questions put to him as to whether or not he knows the meaning and value of an oath, his knowledge of the difference between truth and falsity and the consequences of testifying falsely under oath.

Usually, where mental competence is questioned, expert testimony is taken as to whether or not the witness meets the tests enumerated above. In dealing with a child, the judge questions the child to lay a foundation for the receipt or rejection of his testimony. Expert opinion may also be used in such a case. In both instances, cross-examination is permitted.

The determination of the competency of any witness to testify is a matter solely within the discretion of the judge.

XXIV. PRIVILEGED RELATIONSHIPS

The Civil Practice Law and Rules set forth specific instances ruling that certain communications are privileged and confidential when made under certain circumstances and are inadmissible unless waived.

Professional Persons

A clergyman or other minister of religion shall not be allowed to disclose a confession or other statement made in confidence to him in his professional character, in the course of discipline, enforced by the rules or practice of the religious body to which he belongs.

An attorney or counselor at law shall not be allowed to disclose a communication made to him, or his advice given thereon, in the course of his professional employment; nor shall any clerk, stenographer or other person employed by such attorney or counselor be allowed to disclose any such communication or advice given thereon.

An authorized doctor, dentist, registered nurse or licensed practical nurse shall not be allowed to disclose any information which he or she acquired in attending a patient in a professional capacity, which was necessary to enable him or her to act in that capacity (there are certain exceptions in criminal or identification cases).

The same restrictions apply to registered psychologists and registered and certified social workers.

Waiver

However, waiver of any privilege enumerated herein, may be made by the confessor, client or patient in open court at the trial or proceeding. A paper executed by a party prior thereto providing for such waiver is insufficient as such a waiver. However, attorneys for the respective parties may stipulate for such a waiver prior to the trial. Once the privilege is waived, it is destroyed forever.

Objection

Objection may be raised to disclosure of privileged communications by a party, although the confessor, patient or client is not a party to the action or proceeding. The reason is that it is in the public interest to protect the confidential nature of the relationship.

Husband and Wife

A husband or wife shall not be required, or, without consent of the other, if living, be allowed to disclose a confidential communication made by one to the other during marriage.

If the husband or wife to whom a confidential communication is addressed, makes it public by giving it to another, the confidential character of the communication as against such party is destroyed.

All communications between husband and wife are not incompetent and proper objection must be made on the ground of privilege. However, spouses may testify against each other.

Deceased Persons

Generally, upon a trial or proceeding, a party or person interested in the event, or a person, from, through, or under whom such a party or interested person derives his interest or title, by assignment or otherwise, shall not be examined as a witness in his own behalf or interest, or in behalf of the party succeeding to his title or interest.

Against

The executor, administrator or survivor of a deceased person or a person deriving his title or interest from, through, or under a deceased person, by assignment or otherwise.

Concerning

A personal transaction or communication between the witness and the deceased person.

Except

Where the executor, administrator or survivor so deriving title or interest is examined in his own behalf or the testimony of a deceased person is given in evidence concerning the same transaction or communication.

Waiver

The personal representative of the deceased may waive the privilege by a failure to object on the proper ground, or by calling the survivor to the transaction or communication as a witness; but the testimony is confined strictly to the same transaction or communication.

Lunatics

The same rules of exclusion apply to transactions or communications with a lunatic, where his committee is involved, as apply to deceased persons.

XXV. CREDIBILITY OF WITNESSES AND WEIGHT OF TESTIMONY

General

Credibility of witnesses, the effect and weight of conflicting and contradictory testimony is a question of fact.

Disbelief of Entire Testimony

It is permissible for the trier of the facts to disbelieve the entire testimony of a witness who wilfully testifies to a falsehood as to a material fact.

Weight of Testimony

The weight of testimony on any issue is on that side of the issue on which the evidence is more credible. This is not materially different in meaning from preponderance of evidence.

The number of witnesses, nor their station in life, nor their titles or positions, are controlling.

The testimony of a single witness, if credible, may be sufficient to establish any fact in a civil action.

Interested Witnesses

The testimony of a witness who is interested in the outcome of the action or in any party, may be disbelieved, although it is not otherwise impeached or contradicted.

Disinterested Witness

A disinterested witness is not entitled necessarily to any more credit than an interested witness. As with interested witnesses, it is a matter of credibility. His lack of interest in the outcome may be considered in weighing the credibility of his testimony.

Contradicted Testimony

It is a matter of giving proper weight to testimony when the testimony of a witness is contradicted by himself or other witnesses.

Uncontradicted Testimony

Positive testimony of an uncontradicted witness should not be disregarded arbitrarily.

However, the fact that testimony is uncontradicted, does not make it acceptable, without question, *per se*.

Improbable or Incredible Testimony

Where testimony is extraordinarily in conflict with probability or inconsistent with reason and intelligence, it may be rejected, even though uncontradicted.

Written Against Oral Evidence

Written evidence may be entitled to greater weight than oral testimony given by an interested witness.

Prior Testimony

This is admissible to affect the credibility of a witness' testimony or to show admissions against interest.

XXVI. EXAMINATION OF WITNESSES

Order of Proof

What follows is a short synopsis of the practice and procedure in the civil courts. These may be adapted to administrative hearings.

Generally, this sequence is followed; first, the party holding the affirmative presents his evidence without interruption, except for cross-examination; then the party denying the affirmative submits his evidence without interruption, except for cross-examination; then the party holding the affirmative may offer evidence in rebuttal to the affirmative evidence which the opposite party has introduced.

The order of proof is a matter of discretion with the trier of the facts. He may depart from the foregoing sequence and unless such departure creates prejudice against a party, his discretion is not reviewable on appeal.

The judge may regulate the order in which evidence shall be produced, in permitting the examination of witnesses out of regular order, in allowing the recall of a witness and in relieving a party of his error in not calling a witness at the proper time. He may order some issues to be tried before others are taken up. He may reopen a case to receive additional evidence.

Flexibility may be allowed in the presentation of evidence as a matter of convenience or necessity; for example, because a witness has not appeared on time or the testimony of an expert (such as a doctor) has to be taken out of sequence in order to accommodate him, or presentation of evidence out of regular order may make for more logical sequence or clarity.

Direct Examination

Direct examination is the initial examination of a witness by the party who produces him.

A witness presents what he knows or remembers, without interruption, in answer to questions which should be sufficiently definite and limited as to time. He is then subject to cross-examination (discussed below).

Leading Questions which suggest the answers and virtually put the words into the witness' mouth for him to answer, are improper on examination of a party's own witness.

However, leading questions are permissible to serve a useful purpose, such as introductory matter or to identify the witness. Any such questions must not be prejudicial to the other side.

The outstanding exception to the rule against asking of leading questions is where the witness is hostile, biased or unwilling. It is for the judge to decide whether a witness is hostile, biased or unwilling. If he so decides, the direct examination resembles cross-examination.

Leading questions may be permitted when a witness' recollection has been exhausted, to aid his memory as to dates, names, etc.

Leading questions are permitted where the condition of the witness warrants it, such as in instances of questioning a child, an illiterate, an aged or feeble person or a mentally retarded person.

Leeway is permitted to ask leading questions on cross-examination but only as to matters brought out on direct examination.

The judge may ask leading questions to bring out the true facts, as long as he does not reveal his own opinion in doing so.

Legal Conclusions. A question calling for a legal conclusion is improper.

Intention. Ordinarily, a question should not call for the intention of a witness, aside from what was said or done. An exception to this rule is given under Facts and Opinions, Intentions, in this Appendix on Evidence, *supra.*

Construction of Agreements may not be testified to by a party to a contract, except where there is ambiguity, omission, incompleteness, etc.

Refreshing Recollection. A witness may refresh his memory by the use of any writing, whether made by himself or another. After refreshing his memory, he must testify to facts of his own knowledge. Use of this writing does not necessarily place it in evidence. However, the other side has a right to examine the writing to allow a basis for cross-examination. After this, the other side may offer it in evidence for the trier of the facts to compare the writing with the witness' memory. Where the writing is in great detail, which one would not be expected to commit to memory, the witness may use it to refresh his recollection of its contents.

Conditional Evidence. The judge may allow evidence, subject to connection later. However, if it is not connected before the end of the case, it may be stricken from consideration.

NOTE: This practice is unnecessary in administrative hearings because of the liberal policy of receiving all evidence, with limited exceptions.

XXVII. CROSS-EXAMINATION

Purposes

In brief, such purposes are to discover the truth, and to test the credibility, veracity, accuracy and mental capacity of a witness. It is an examination for the purpose of clarifying evidence and to correct omissions.

Official Reports, Certificates or Statements

Where an official report, certificate or other written statement is received in evidence, and it appears that such report, etc., plays a substantial part in arriving at a just and informed decision, and it is reasonably practicable to do so, the author thereof should be produced for cross-examination.

Control

The manner and the extent of cross-examination lies largely within the discretion of the trier of the case.

However, the cross-examination of adverse witnesses is a matter of right in every trial of a disputed issue of fact. Denial of such right is serious error.

Cross-examination may be pursued as a matter of right, so far as it relates to facts in issue or other relevant facts.

Collateral Matters

If the cross-examination concerns collateral matters, the cross-examiner is bound by the answers given. In such cross-examination, the cross-examiner, in effect makes the adverse witness his own witness as to such collateral matters. He may not refute or contradict such collateral testimony by calling other witnesses or by producing other evidence to contradict it.

Impeaching Own Witness

Ordinarily, a party calling a witness to testify in his behalf, vouches for his credibility and may not impeach or contradict his testimony.

However, where an examiner is honestly surprised or disappointed by unexpected testimony of his own witness, he may interrogate him as to previous statements made by him, either oral or written, which are inconsistent with his present testimony, in order to refresh his memory or elicit an explanation of his inconsistency. The same practice is permitted when a cross-examination concerns collateral matters, where the cross-examiner makes an adverse witness his own.

Leeway is permitted in asking leading questions on cross-examination.

Hostile Witnesses

Calling an adversary as a witness does not mean that his credibility is vouched for. He is regarded as a hostile witness.

The hostility of a witness may be proven by any competent evidence. If a witness denies his hostility, other witnesses may be called to show affirmative acts or declarations of hostility.

Prior Inconsistent Statements

Whether made in court under oath or outside of court, orally or in writing, prior inconsistent statements may be introduced to impeach the credibility of a witness.

Rebuttal

Rebuttal evidence is evidence in denial of affirmative facts the answering party has sought to establish.

Conviction of a Crime

Prior convictions of a crime of a witness are proper subjects of cross-examination to affect his credibility. However, such a person is a competent witness. Only his credibility is involved.

Privilege of Witness Against Self-Incrimination

The Civil Practice Law and Rules provide that a witness is not required to give an answer which will tend to accuse himself of a crime or to expose him to a penalty or forfeiture.

A witness may not be compelled to answer, if he claims that the answer will tend to incriminate or degrade him.

A witness has the privilege against self-incrimination on constitutional grounds. A witness must invoke this privilege himself but a party may invoke the privilege through his attorney.

Upon service of a subpoena *duces tecum,* a witness has a legal right to refuse to produce his private books and records, or to testify regarding them, if such books and records or testimony would tend to incriminate him.

However, upon service of a subpoena *duces tecum,* a corporate officer must produce corporate books and records, even though they might tend to incriminate him and/or the corporation. If his testimony would tend to incriminate the corporation but not him personally, he cannot refuse to testify.

Waiver of Privilege

The privilege against self-incrimination is waived by failure to assert it at the commencement of the examination dealing with incriminating matters. Where the privilege is waived, the waiver applies only to the action, proceeding or hearing in which it occurs.

Re-Examination

A witness may be recalled for re-examination for the purpose of explaining any new facts brought out on cross-examination.

Re-examination is in the discretion of the trier of the case.

XXVIII. PRODUCTION OF DOCUMENTS

The trier of the case has the power to direct the production of any documents, papers, etc., which are within the trial room, so long as the person having them could have been compelled to produce them by service of a subpoena *duces tecum,* subject to the rules on privilege between attorney and client.

XXIX. OBJECTIONS

Generally, the trier of the case may receive all evidence offered, unless proper objection is made by the opposing party. In his discretion, he may exclude improper evidence without objection being taken.

It is the function of an objection to give the trier of the case and the opposing party the opportunity to prevent or correct an error in the conduct of the case.

The office of an objection is to stop an answer. Objection should be made the instant the evidence is offered. If not, it is usually waived, unless the witness answered so quickly, there was no time to object. In the latter event, if the objection is sustained, the answer should be disregarded.

An objection should be made upon specific grounds to enable a proper ruling to be made and to enable the opposing party to resort to some other proper form of proof.

Taking Exceptions

Formal exceptions to the rulings of the court are unnecessary. It is deemed taken by the party adversely affected by the ruling, provided he has made his position known to the court by objection to the evidence or in any other way.

XXX. WAIVER OF RULE OF EVIDENCE

Parties may waive a rule of evidence. However, the evidence so received must be considered by the trier of the case for what it is worth.

XXXI. CHARACTER EVIDENCE

Generally, evidence of the character of a party or witness in a civil case cannot be offered as evidence that he did or did not do an act charged. It is usually immaterial and inadmissible.

However, if the plaintiff's pleadings allege good character and reputation and the defendant's answer denies these allegations, the evidence of good character is put in issue and the plaintiff may thereupon seek to prove his good character and reputation.

Where a party or witness admits that he was convicted of a crime, he may thereafter offer evidence of witnesses as to his general reputation in the community.

A character witness may be asked whether he knows the general reputation of the person among his neighbors and what that reputation is.

CRIMINAL INVESTIGATION

TECHNIQUE OF INTERVIEWS AND INTERROGATION

CONTENTS

CRIMINAL INVESTIGATION

TECHNIQUE OF INTERVIEWS AND INTERROGATION

---

1. GENERAL

The successful investigation of criminal offenses depends in a great measure upon the effective questioning of complainants, witnesses, informants, suspects, and other persons encountered during the course of an investigation. Questioning is divided into two broad classifications: *interviews*, which are conducted to learn facts from persons who may have knowledge of a wrongful act but who are not themselves implicated; and *interrogations*, which are conducted to learn facts and to obtain admissions or confessions of wrongful acts from persons who are implicated in a wrongful act. Persons who have been interviewed may later be interrogated. An interrogation is not necessarily confined to individuals suspected of criminal acts, but may include persons who may have been accessories, or who may have knowledge of the crime which, for various motives, they are reluctant to admit. It is usually advisable to take statements from persons being interviewed or interrogated. When an interview or interrogation develops information which will have definite value as evidence, that information or evidence must be recorded in a written, signed, and witnessed statement, or preserved through mechanical recording.

2. PURPOSE OF INTERVIEW

An interview is an informal questioning to learn facts. The successful investigation of crime requires that the investigator be able to learn, through personal questioning, what the person interviewed has observed through his five senses: sight, hearing, taste, smell, and touch. Each individual interviewed is presumed to possess certain information that may lead to the solution of a crime. Effective interviewing requires that the interviewer make full use of all the knowledge of human nature he possesses, so that the individual interviewed will disclose all that he knows about the matter in question. If a person does not possess knowledge of the crime, the interview should establish that fact. Pertinent negative evidence is as much a part of a complete investigation as positive information.

3. PREPARATION FOR INTERVIEW

Interviews other than those conducted at the scene of the crime should be planned carefully and thoroughly to prevent repetition of the interview. The investigator must review thoroughly all developments in the investigation prior to the interview. He must also consider the relationship of the person to be interviewed to the investigation; i. e., complainant, victim, witness, or informant. An effective interviewer combines his knowledge of human nature with all available information about the person to be interviewed, such as education, character, reputation, associates, habits, and past criminal record. This background information is used advantageously in the interview. The investigator should estimate the extent and kind of information which he may expect to elicit. He should prepare, by noting pertinent facts to be developed, to detect inconsistencies and discrepancies in the statements of the person being interviewed, to evaluate them, and to require their clarification. The investigator should prepare a plan for the interview which takes into consideration the information available to him about the person to be interviewed; the time, place, and environment for the interview; as well as the legal proof to be developed in the crime.

4. TIME OF INTERVIEW

An interview should be conducted as soon as possible after the discovery of a crime. The investigator should take as much time as is required for a complete and thorough interview.

5. PLACE OF INTERVIEW

When possible, the place of the interview should be so selected as to assure a favorable environment. When possible, the interview should be conducted in a comfortable room and in an environment familiar to the person interviewed. The person to be interviewed should never be brought to the investigator.

6. INTRODUCTION OF THE INVESTIGATOR

Usually the investigator and the person to be interviewed are strangers. The investigator should introduce himself, present his credentials (when appropriate), and begin by making a general statement regarding the purpose of the interview. The introduction should be made in such a manner as to establish a cordial relationship between the investigator and the person being interviewed.

7. CONTROL OVER INTERVIEWS

An investigator must maintain absolute control of the interview at all times. He must be careful not to elicit false information through improper questioning. He may permit digression or discussion of matters seemingly unrelated to the crime in order to place the person interviewed at ease but he must not permit the person being interviewed to become evasive. If the person interviewed should become so evasive as to obscure the purpose of the interview, effective results may be obtained by a more formal type of questioning, taking notes, or by the aggressiveness of the investigator.

8. RIGHTS OF PERSON INTERVIEWED

Although an investigator has no legal power to compel a person being interviewed to divulge information, he may, if he is clever and alert, induce him to disclose what he knows. When an interview develops into an interrogation, the investigator must warn the person being interviewed of his rights (par. 26).

9. ATTITUDE AND DEMEANOR OF INVESTIGATOR

The attitude and demeanor of an investigator contributes immeasurably to the success or failure of an interview. The investigator should be friendly, yet businesslike. He should endeavor to lead the person being interviewed into talkativeness. He should then direct the conversation toward the investigation. The individual being interviewed should be permitted to give an uninterrupted account while the investigator makes mental notes of omissions, inconsistencies, or discrepancies that require clarification by later questioning. The investigator should strive to turn to advantage the subject's prejudices. He rarely reveals the precise objective of an interview, and usually obtains a more accurate account from the person interviewed if he claims only to be attempting to establish facts. He should avoid a clash of personalities; acts of undue familiarity: the use of profanity or violent expressions such as "kill," "steal," "confess," "murder"; improbable stories; or distracting mannerisms such as pacing the floor or fumbling with objects.

10. TYPES OF APPROACHES

The *indirect* approach employed in interviewing consists of discussion carried on in a conversational tone that permits the person being interviewed to talk without having to answer direct questions. The *direct* approach consists of direct questioning as in interrogations (par. 28a).The use of interrogation technique often succeeds when the person interviewed fears or dislikes police officers, fears retribution from a criminal, desires to protect a friend or relative, is impudent, or, for diverse reasons, is unwilling to cooperate with the investigator. Unreliable persons or liars should always be permitted to give their version of an incident. They may, through contradiction or denial, trip themselves into admissions through which the true facts may be obtained. When interviewing shy or nervous persons, the investigator may be obliged to obtain information piecemeal. He should interview in the normal environment of such persons and should be as casual and calm as possible. The talkative person should be allowed to speak freely and to use his own expressions, but should be confined to the subject by appropriate questions. When persons pretend to know nothing about an incident, the investigator should ask many questions, any one which, if answered, will refute their claim that they know nothing at all. Disinterested persons may divulge more information if their personal interest can be aroused by an indirect approach. Investigators should always attempt to put uneducated witnesses at ease and to help them express themselves as best they can, but should not put words into their mouths. Flattery is most often successful when alcoholics or braggarts are interviewed. Information gained from such individuals must be corroborated.

11. INTERVIEW OF COMPLAINANTS

In interviewing complainants, the investigator should be considerate, understanding, tactful, and impartial, regardless of the motive for the complaint, and should inform the complainant that appropriate action will be initiated promptly.

12. INTERVIEW OF VICTIMS

When interviewing victims, the investigator must consider their emotional state, particularly in crimes of violence. Frequently, victims have unsupported beliefs regarding the circumstances connected with the crime. Their observations may be partial and imperfect because of excitement and tension. It is imperative that the investigator obtain from the victim an accurate account of the circumstances that existed immediately before, during, and after the incident. The investigator should consider the reputation of the victim in determining the credibility of his complaint.

13. INTERVIEW OF WITNESSES

The investigator must frequently assist witnesses to recall and relate facts exactly as they observed them. He must know what may affect a person's ability to observe and describe acts, articles, or circumstances related to a crime (ch. 3). He should lead witnesses toward accurate statements of fact by assisting them to recall in detail their experiences.

14. TYPES OF WITNESSES

In general, children from 7 to 12 years of age are good observers, although their testimony may be inadmissible in court. Teen-age children are also good observers but may exaggerate. Young adults are often poor witnesses; middle-aged and older persons are the best witnesses. Persons differ in their physical and mental characteristics as well as in their experience and training. These differences may cause them to notice only those aspects of a situation in which they may have had a particular experience. As a consequence, they differ in their observations, interpretations, and descriptions. If a witness cannot recall what he has observed, poor memory may be the cause. Preoccupation of a witness may often prevent him from recalling exactly what occurred. Lack of education may make it difficult for a witness to describe what he observed; such a person is sometimes reluctant to divulge information because of embarrassment over his diction. That which has been observed, because of exaggeration, misrepresentation, or inaccurate interpretation, may result in faulty information; i. e., a squeal of joy may be misinterpreted as a scream of terror. The emotions of witnesses before, during, and after an incident, and when interviewed, greatly affect their recall of events as they actually occurred. A frightened witness may recall events differently than a calm, unruffled person. Witnesses may exaggerate more each time their observations are repeated.

15. ASSISTANCE TO WITNESSES IN DESCRIPTIONS

The investigator should provide certain indexes to assist witnesses in describing size, height, weight, distance, and colors. The eye-level method of determining height may be used as standard. By asking a witness to tell how far another person's eyes were above or below his own, the investigator may obtain an estimate of height. Speed is difficult to estimate accurately; even opinions based on long experience may be subject to influence by noise, light, weather, and other conditions. Age is difficult for witnesses to judge because of differences among races, nationalities, and individuals; if selected individuals are used for comparison, they must be chosen carefully. In situations which are strange or which involve unusual circumstances, the witness may have no standards or associations on which to base his judgment and may be unable to utilize the standards presented for comparison. A detailed review or reconstruction of events will sometimes help the witness to recall events, but the investigator must be careful to avoid confusing the actual event with the reconstruction.

16. CREDIBILITY OF WITNESSES

Credibility of a witness is usually governed by his character and is evidenced by his reputation for veracity. Personal or financial reason or previous criminal activity may cause a witness to give false information to avoid being implicated. Hope of gain by informants or prisoners; political, racial, or religious factors; and hatred for the police or the suspect are some of the reasons why a witness may make a false statement. Age, sex, physical and mental abnormalities, loyalty, revenge, social and economic status, indulgence in alcohol, and the influence of other persons are some of the many factors which may affect the accuracy, willingness, or ability with which witnesses observe, interpret, and describe occurrences.

17. EVALUATION DURING INTERVIEW

During an interview, the investigator must evaluate continuously the mannerisms and the emotional state of the person in terms of the information developed. The manner in which a person relates his story or answers questions may indicate that he is not telling the truth or is concealing information. Evasiveness, hesitation, or unwillingness to discuss situations may signify a lack of cooperation. The relation of body movements to the emotional state of persons must be carefully considered by the investigator. A dry mouth indicated by the wetting of the lips, fidgeting, or vague movements of the hands may indicate nervousness or deception. A "cold sweat" or pale face may indicate fear. A slight gasp, holding the breath, or an unsteady voice may indicate that the knowledge of the investigator has shocked the person being interviewed. The pumping of the heart may be observed by the pulse in the neck. A ruddy or flushed face may be an indication of anger or embarrassment, not necessarily guilt, and may also indicate that the matter under discussion is of vital importance, or that some information is being withheld. Although such symptoms are not necessarily valid indications of guilt or innocence and may be a manifestation of the physical condition or health of the individual, they are often related to the emotional state of the person.

18. INTERVIEW NOTES

Complete notes are essential to effective investigation and reporting. Normally, most people have no objection to note-taking; however, the investigator should not take notes until he has had an opportunity to gage the person's reactions, since note-taking may create a reluctance to divulge information. If he does not take notes, the investigator should record, at the first opportunity after the interview, all pertinent information while it is fresh in his mind. Notes on interviews should contain the case number; hour, date, and place of interview; complete identification of the person interviewed; names of other persons present; and a resumé of the interview.

19. PURPOSE OF INTERROGATION

The interrogation should take place immediately if the suspect is surprised or apprehended in the act of committing a crime. In all other instances, interrogation should be conducted only after sufficient information has been secured and the background of the suspect has been thoroughly explored. The purpose of interrogation of a suspect is to obtain an admission or confession of his wrongful acts and a written, signed, and witnessed statement, and to establish the facts of a crime or to develop information which will enable the investigator to obtain direct, physical, or other evidence to prove or disprove the truth of an admission or confession. A confession is an acknowledgment of guilt, whereas an admission is a self-incriminatory statement falling short of an acknowledgment of guilt. The securing of confessions or acknowledgments of guilt does not complete the investigation of a crime. A statement made by one conspirator during the conspiracy and in pursuance of it is admissible in evidence against his co-conspirators as tending to prove the fact of the matter stated. In interrogation, the investigator seeks to learn the identity of accomplices and details of any other crime in which the suspect may have been involved.

20. PREPARATION FOR INTERROGATION

a. Preparation for interrogation should be thorough. The investigator should base his plan for interrogation on background data, information, or direct evidence received from victims and witnesses, physical evidence, and reconstruction of the crime scene. The plan, which should be written, should take into consideration the various means for testing the truthfulness of the suspect and for gaining a psychological advantage over him through the use of known facts and proper use of time, place, and environment. Unless the investigator interrogates a suspect immediately following the commission of a crime, or desires to question him without previous notification, he should be interrogated at criminal investigation headquarters, where recordings may be made or stenographic notes may be taken.

b. During interrogation, the subject should be seated in a plain chair placed where his movements and physical reactions may be observed easily. The interrogation room should be plainly but comfortably furnished, without items which may cause distraction. Recording devices, one-way mirrors, and similar equipment should appear as normal furnishings. Tables, desks, and other furnishings should be located where they will not impair the interrogator's observation of the suspect.

21. CLASSIFICATION OF SUSPECTS

Background information and the facts established in an investigation enable the investigator to classify persons to be interrogated as follows:

a. Known offenders, whose guilt is reasonably certain on the basis of the evidence available.

b. Persons whose guilt is doubtful or uncertain because of the evidence or lack of evidence.

c. Material witnesses, accessories, and persons who have knowledge of the crime but may not themselves be guilty of a crime. Persons to be interrogated may be further classified as those readily influenced by sympathy or understanding; and those readily influenced by the use of an attitude of suspicion and obvious disbelief.

22. LENGTH OF INTERROGATION

No time limit is placed on the duration of interrogation except that it shall not be so long and under such conditions as to amount to duress. Questioning for many hours without food, sleep, or under glaring lights has been held to constitute such duress as to invalidate a confession. The suspect may be questioned at length in an attempt to break down his resistance, or he may be questioned for short periods daily as a test of his consistency. The interrogator should always consider the physical condition of the person being interrogated as well as his emotional stability. Once the suspect has begun to reveal pertinent information, the interrogation should not be interrupted.

23. PERSONS AT INTERROGATION

An interrogation usually should be conducted in complete privacy. A person under interrogation is not inclined to reveal confidences to a public gathering. Witnesses to a confession may be called in to hear the reading of the statement and the declaration that it is the subject's statement, to witness the signing by the subject, and to affix their own signatures. Some investigative agencies advocate the presence of a witness at all times during an interrogation, particularly during the period of warning of rights and at such other periods when corroborative testimony might be needed or desirable. When a woman is questioned, the interrogator should provide witnesses, preferably women, in order to avoid charges of compromise which an unscrupulous woman may later interject as mitigating circumstance.

24. INTERROGATION CHECKLIST

Before beginning an interrogation, the investigator should check his preparation against the following questions:

a. Has the crime scene been carefully and adequately searched for real evidence?

b. Have all persons known to have knowledge of the crime been questioned?

c. Has all possible evidence been obtained?

d. Has the person to be interrogated been searched?

e. Have all files been checked for pertinent information?

f. Is background investigation complete?

g. Is the interrogation room properly prepared for the interrogation?

h. Is the interrogation plan complete?

i. Have the elements of legal proof been checked?

j. Are all details of the investigation firmly fixed in the investigator's mind?

k. What information should be elicited from the individual to be interrogated?

25. INTRODUCTION OF INVESTIGATOR

Prior to any interrogation, the investigator may introduce and identify himself by presenting his credentials if the person to be interrogated questions the authority of the investigator. After the introduction, the person to be interrogated should be informed in general terms of the nature of the investigation being conducted. The investigator, however, should not disclose his knowledge of the case, nor should he prematurely disclose any fact of the case.

26. RIGHTS OF PERSON BEING INTERROGATED

The investigator should begin interrogation by explaining to the person to be questioned his rights under the Fifth Amendment to the Constitution of the United States, if he is a civilian, and under Article 31 of the Uniform Code of Military Justice, if he is a military person. The person to be questioned is informed that he need not answer any question which may tend to incriminate him but that, if he chooses to answer any question, such answer may be used in testimony against him. Throughout the questioning the investigator must refrain from threats, violence, or promise of reward. In response to a request by the person being questioned for legal counsel, the investigator should courteously but firmly refuse and state that the Uniform Code of Military Justice does not provide for counsel prior to charges being preferred against a soldier.

27. ATTITUDE OF INVESTIGATOR

Because of the importance of admissions or confessions, the investigator must become skilled in the art of interrogation. He must master a variety of questioning techniques, learn to judge the psychological strength or weakness of others, and learn to take advantage of his own particular abilities in questioning any suspect or reluctant witness. He must not presume guilt of the persons being interrogated without sufficient proof. He must act as naturally as possible under the circumstances. If a suspect begins admitting criminal acts, the investigator must not become overeager or condescending. The interrogator should, when it is necessary to stir the emotions of another to confess a wrongful act, permit his own emotions to be stirred.

28. TYPES OF APPROACH

He adapts his approach to the character and background of the person to be interrogated, the known facts of the crime, and the real evidence available. The investigator may use any of the following type approaches or any combination of them:

a. The *direct approach* is normally employed where guilt is reasonably certain. The investigator assumes an air of confidence concerning the guilt of the offender and points out the evidence indicative of guilt. He outwardly sympathizes with the offender and indicates that anyone else might have done the same thing under similar circumstances. He urges the offender to tell the whole truth, avoids threatening words or insinuation, and develops a detailed account of the crime from premeditation to commission. He may ask questions such as the following: "Tell me all you know about this. When did you get the idea of doing it? Why did you do it? How did you do that? Where did you get the money?" In dealing with habitual criminals whose guilt is reasonably certain and who apparently have no feeling of wrongdoing, the investigator must convince them that their guilt can be or is established by the testimony of witnesses or available evidence. Investigators must never make promises of leniency or clemency as these promises might vitiate confessions obtained as a result of the interrogation.

b. The *indirect approach* is normally employed in interrogating a person who has knowledge of the crime. The investigator must proceed cautiously.

He requests the individual being interrogated to tell all he knows about the incident. He then requires an explanation of discrepancies or distortions and endeavors to lead the individual being interrogated into admissions of truth. When facts indicative of guilt are developed, the investigator casually asks questions to determine through the offender's reactions whether he will acknowledge or deny guilt. When guilt appears probable, the investigator reverts to direct questioning to obtain an admission or confession.

c. The *emotional approach* is designed to arouse any play upon the emotions of a person. Body actions may indicate the presence of nervous tension. The investigator points out these signs of nervous tension to the person under interrogation. The investigator may discuss the moral seriousness of the offense, emphasize the penalty, and appeal to the suspect's pride or ego, fear, like or dislike, or his hate and desire for revenge. This approach may lead to emotional breakdown and a confession.

d. *Subterfuge* is employed to induce guilty persons to confess when all other approaches have failed. Considerable care should be exercised in the employment of subterfuge. If the person to be interrogated recognizes the approach as subterfuge, further efforts to obtain an admission or confession may be futile. Examples of subterfuge are:

(1) *Hypothetical story.* A fictitious crime, varying only in minute details from the offense of which the subject is suspected, is related to him. The investigator later visits the subject and asks him to write out details of the hypothetical story as related. If the

subject is guilty, he often includes details of the crime under investigation, but not mentioned by the investigator in his fictitious story. When confronted with these inconsistencies, the suspect may make a confession.

(2) *Signed false statement.* When evidence indicates, but is not conclusive, that a certain person may be guilty of a crime, he may be requested to make a sworn written statement. After he has made a false written statement, the discrepancies contained therein are pointed out to him in an attempt to gain a true confession.

(3) '*Cold shoulder.*" This term designates a technique of subterfuge keynoted by indifference. The person suspected is invited to come to the investigator's office. If he accepts the invitation, he is taken either to the office or the crime scene. The investigator, or those accompanying the person subjected to this type of interrogation, say nothing to him or to each other, and await his reactions. This technique may cause the suspect to surmise that the investigator has evidence adequate to prove his guilt.

(4) *Playing one suspect against another.* When two or more persons are suspected of having been involved in a crime, the person believed to have the weakest character is interrogated first. The others are interrogated separately and informed that their partner has accused them of the crime. A confession, shown to the others involved, may influence

them to attempt to protect themselves by confessing.

(5) *Contrasting personalities.* This technique employs two investigators, one determined and the other sympathetic and understanding. The interrogation is so arranged that the person under interrogation will play into the hands of one or the other.

29. INTERROGATION NOTES

The taking of notes during an interrogation may be essential in order to record all pertinent information; however, the effect of note-taking on the success of the interrogation must be considered. If notes are not taken during the interrogation, the investigator should record all pertinent data immediately after the interrogation.

30. SCIENTIFIC AIDS TO INTERROGATION

Scientific aids are available to the investigator to assist in the investigation of criminal offenses. These aids are normally employed to develop information from persons who are suspected of committing a crime. They may also be used to check the validity and completeness of information given by complainants, witnesses, and victims.

31. LIE DETECTING SET

Lie detecting set examinations can be conducted only by operators trained in the use of the instrument. The lie detecting set is an instrument which records the body changes that accompany emotions and is used to develop information, to determine if a person has knowledge of an offense, and to obtain an admission or confession of guilt. The provisions of Article 31, Uniform Code of Military Justice, and the Fifth Amendment to the Constitution of the United States apply to persons who are requested to submit to an examination by a lie detecting set. Investigators should obtain written consent from all persons subjected to lie detecting set examinations, acknowledging that they have been informed of their rights and that they agree to submit voluntarily to such an examination. A copy of this statement should be included in the case file folder. In general, graphs obtained during a lie detecting set examination are not admissible as evidence in court. However, the operator is usually permitted to testify relative to the questions asked, and the answers given. Oral or written admissions or confessions obtained as a consequence of the examination may be admitted into evidence, if they meet legal requirements.

32. NARCO-ANALYSIS

Narco-analysis is the term employed to define the questioning of a person under the influence of drugs (truth serums). Scopolamine, sodium amytal, and sodium pentathol are the drugs most commonly used. When properly administered, these drugs tend to overcome inhibitions. The use of narco-analysis as an investigative technique has not found general acceptance. Admissions or confessions obtained through the use of truth serums are not admissible as evidence in court. The information obtained may be used only to develop the investigation. The subject must be warned of his rights, and a written statement obtained wherein the subject acknowledges the warning and voluntarily agrees to the narco-analysis. *No person may be compelled to submit to such an examination. It must be conducted only when a qualified medical officer is available to administer the drugs and to witness the examination.*

ANSWER SHEET

TEST NO. ________ PART ______ TITLE OF POSITION ____________________
(AS GIVEN IN EXAMINATION ANNOUNCEMENT - INCLUDE OPTION, IF ANY)

PLACE OF EXAMINATION ____________________ (CITY OR TOWN) ________ (STATE) DATE ________

RATING

USE THE SPECIAL PENCIL. MAKE GLOSSY BLACK MARKS.

1 A B C D E	26 A B C D E	51 A B C D E	76 A B C D E	101 A B C D E
2 A B C D E	27 A B C D E	52 A B C D E	77 A B C D E	102 A B C D E
3 A B C D E	28 A B C D E	53 A B C D E	78 A B C D E	103 A B C D E
4 A B C D E	29 A B C D E	54 A B C D E	79 A B C D E	104 A B C D E
5 A B C D E	30 A B C D E	55 A B C D E	80 A B C D E	105 A B C D E
6 A B C D E	31 A B C D E	56 A B C D E	81 A B C D E	106 A B C D E
7 A B C D E	32 A B C D E	57 A B C D E	82 A B C D E	107 A B C D E
8 A B C D E	33 A B C D E	58 A B C D E	83 A B C D E	108 A B C D E
9 A B C D E	34 A B C D E	59 A B C D E	84 A B C D E	109 A B C D E
10 A B C D E	35 A B C D E	60 A B C D E	85 A B C D E	110 A B C D E

Make only ONE mark for each answer. Additional and stray marks may be counted as mistakes. In making corrections, erase errors COMPLETELY.

11 A B C D E	36 A B C D E	61 A B C D E	86 A B C D E	111 A B C D E
12 A B C D E	37 A B C D E	62 A B C D E	87 A B C D E	112 A B C D E
13 A B C D E	38 A B C D E	63 A B C D E	88 A B C D E	113 A B C D E
14 A B C D E	39 A B C D E	64 A B C D E	89 A B C D E	114 A B C D E
15 A B C D E	40 A B C D E	65 A B C D E	90 A B C D E	115 A B C D E
16 A B C D E	41 A B C D E	66 A B C D E	91 A B C D E	116 A B C D E
17 A B C D E	42 A B C D E	67 A B C D E	92 A B C D E	117 A B C D E
18 A B C D E	43 A B C D E	68 A B C D E	93 A B C D E	118 A B C D E
19 A B C D E	44 A B C D E	69 A B C D E	94 A B C D E	119 A B C D E
20 A B C D E	45 A B C D E	70 A B C D E	95 A B C D E	120 A B C D E
21 A B C D E	46 A B C D E	71 A B C D E	96 A B C D E	121 A B C D E
22 A B C D E	47 A B C D E	72 A B C D E	97 A B C D E	122 A B C D E
23 A B C D E	48 A B C D E	73 A B C D E	98 A B C D E	123 A B C D E
24 A B C D E	49 A B C D E	74 A B C D E	99 A B C D E	124 A B C D E
25 A B C D E	50 A B C D E	75 A B C D E	100 A B C D E	125 A B C D E

ANSWER SHEET

TEST NO. ____________ PART ________ TITLE OF POSITION ______________________________
(AS GIVEN IN EXAMINATION ANNOUNCEMENT - INCLUDE OPTION, IF ANY)

PLACE OF EXAMINATION ______________________ (CITY OR TOWN) ______________________ (STATE) DATE ____________

RATING

USE THE SPECIAL PENCIL. MAKE GLOSSY BLACK MARKS.

1	A B C D E	26	A B C D E	51	A B C D E	76	A B C D E	101	A B C D E
2	A B C D E	27	A B C D E	52	A B C D E	77	A B C D E	102	A B C D E
3	A B C D E	28	A B C D E	53	A B C D E	78	A B C D E	103	A B C D E
4	A B C D E	29	A B C D E	54	A B C D E	79	A B C D E	104	A B C D E
5	A B C D E	30	A B C D E	55	A B C D E	80	A B C D E	105	A B C D E
6	A B C D E	31	A B C D E	56	A B C D E	81	A B C D E	106	A B C D E
7	A B C D E	32	A B C D E	57	A B C D E	82	A B C D E	107	A B C D E
8	A B C D E	33	A B C D E	58	A B C D E	83	A B C D E	108	A B C D E
9	A B C D E	34	A B C D E	59	A B C D E	84	A B C D E	109	A B C D E
10	A B C D E	35	A B C D E	60	A B C D E	85	A B C D E	110	A B C D E

Make only ONE mark for each answer. Additional and stray marks may be counted as mistakes. In making corrections, erase errors COMPLETELY.

11	A B C D E	36	A B C D E	61	A B C D E	86	A B C D E	111	A B C D E
12	A B C D E	37	A B C D E	62	A B C D E	87	A B C D E	112	A B C D E
13	A B C D E	38	A B C D E	63	A B C D E	88	A B C D E	113	A B C D E
14	A B C D E	39	A B C D E	64	A B C D E	89	A B C D E	114	A B C D E
15	A B C D E	40	A B C D E	65	A B C D E	90	A B C D E	115	A B C D E
16	A B C D E	41	A B C D E	66	A B C D E	91	A B C D E	116	A B C D E
17	A B C D E	42	A B C D E	67	A B C D E	92	A B C D E	117	A B C D E
18	A B C D E	43	A B C D E	68	A B C D E	93	A B C D E	118	A B C D E
19	A B C D E	44	A B C D E	69	A B C D E	94	A B C D E	119	A B C D E
20	A B C D E	45	A B C D E	70	A B C D E	95	A B C D E	120	A B C D E
21	A B C D E	46	A B C D E	71	A B C D E	96	A B C D E	121	A B C D E
22	A B C D E	47	A B C D E	72	A B C D E	97	A B C D E	122	A B C D E
23	A B C D E	48	A B C D E	73	A B C D E	98	A B C D E	123	A B C D E
24	A B C D E	49	A B C D E	74	A B C D E	99	A B C D E	124	A B C D E
25	A B C D E	50	A B C D E	75	A B C D E	100	A B C D E	125	A B C D E